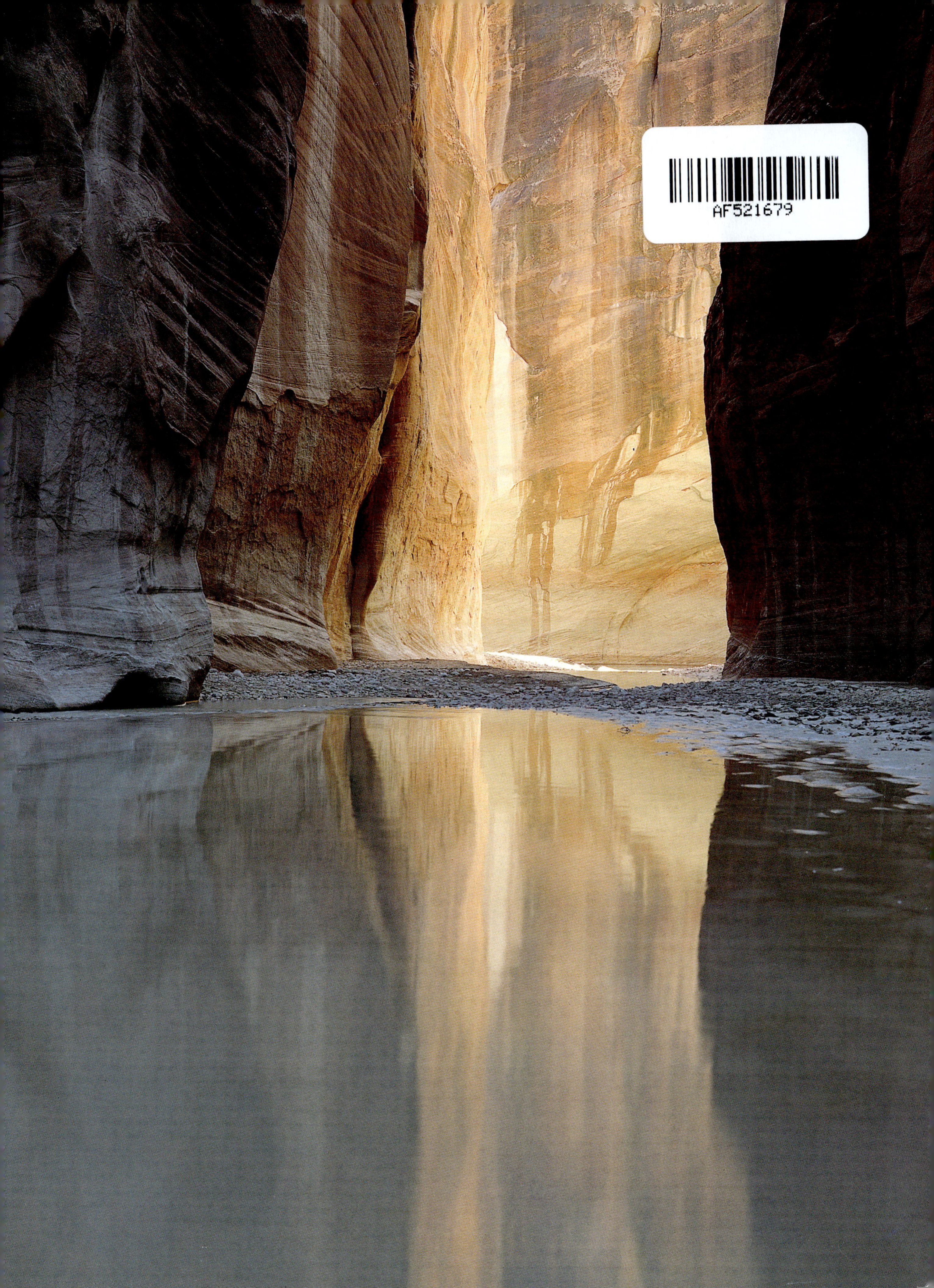

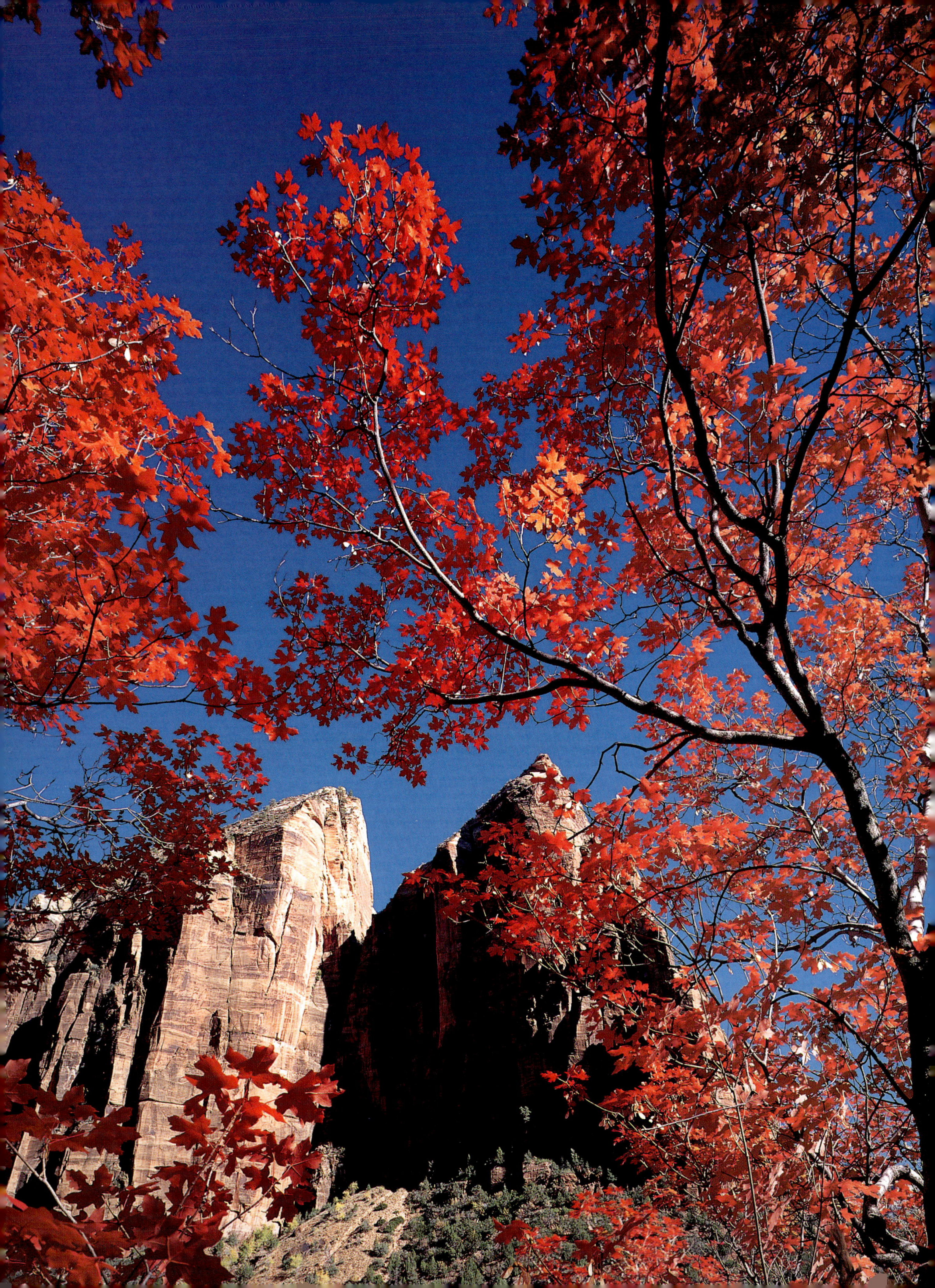

PORTRAIT OF

UTAH

DAVID MUENCH

Text by Ann Zwinger

GRAPHIC ARTS CENTER PUBLISHING®

International Standard Book Number 1-55868-423-9
Library of Congress Catalog Number 98-89045

An imprint of Graphic Arts Center Publishing Company
P.O. Box 10306, Portland, OR 97296-0306
503-226-2402

President/Publisher • Charles M. Hopkins
Editorial Staff • Douglas A. Pfeiffer, Ellen Harkins Wheat, Timothy W. Frew,
Diana S. Eilers, Jean Andrews, Alicia I. Paulson, Joanna Goebel, Deborah J. Loop
Production Staff • Richard L. Owsiany, Lauren Taylor
Cartographer • Manoa Mapworks, Inc.
Book Manufacturing • Lincoln & Allen Company
Printed and bound in the United States of America

FRONT COVER: AQUA CANYON, BRYCE CANYON NATIONAL PARK.

BACK COVER: POOL IN NARROWS, WHITE CANYON.

HALF TITLE PAGE: PARIA CANYON, VERMILLION CLIFFS WILDERNESS.

FRONTISPIECE: THREE PATRIARCHS IN AUTUMN, ZION NATIONAL PARK.

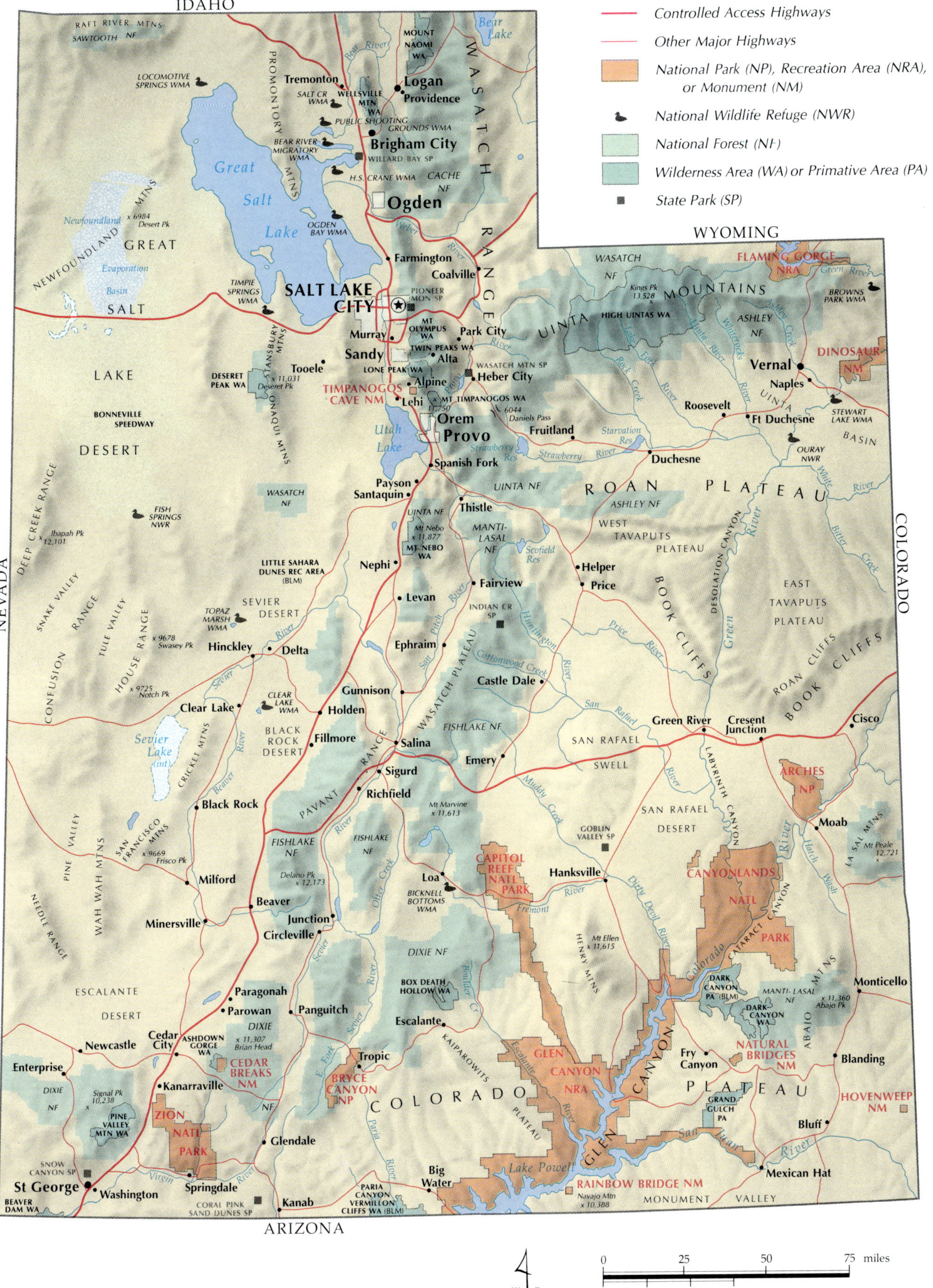

Elevation in Feet

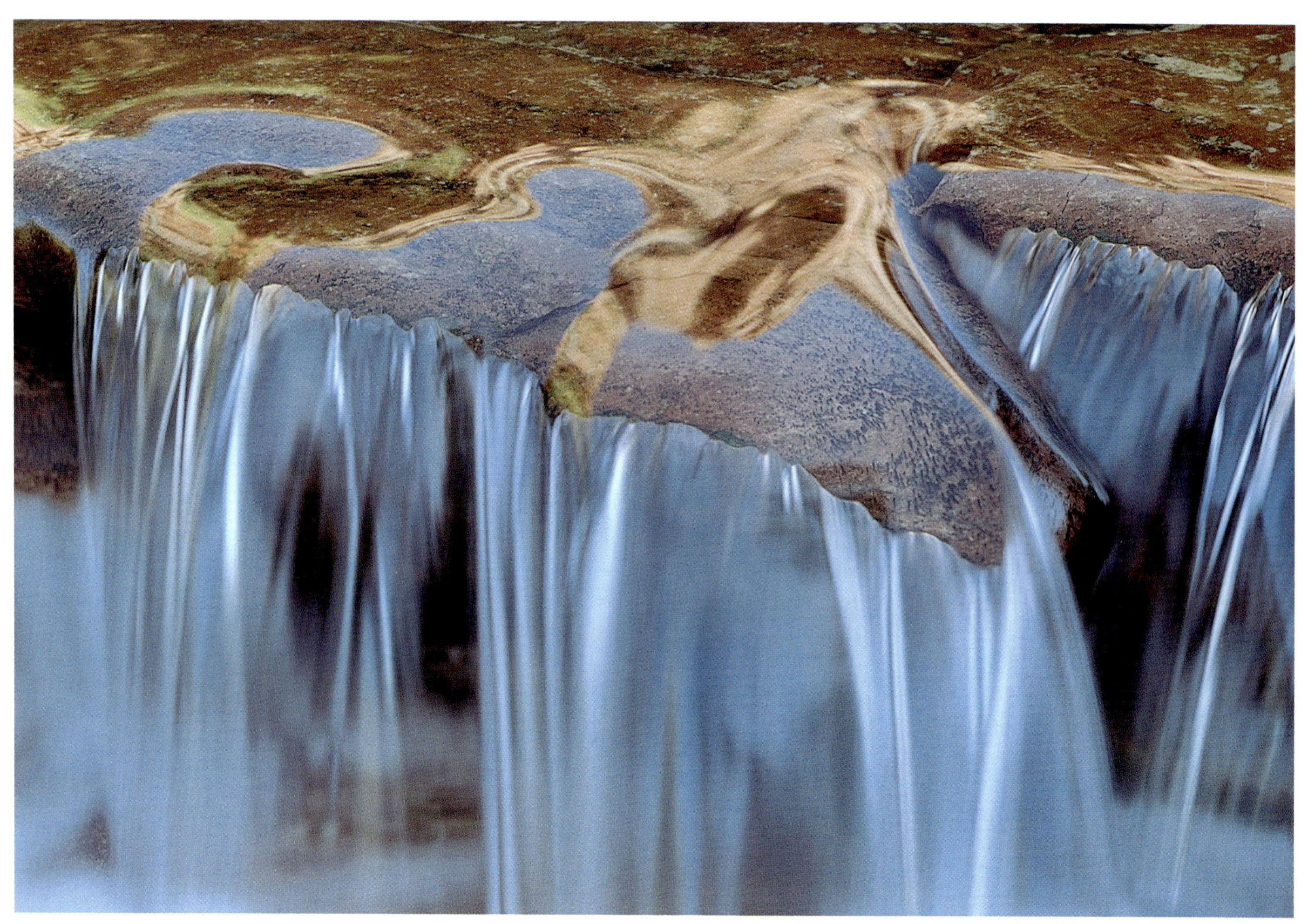

ABOVE: NORTH GUARDIAN ANGEL REFLECTS IN NORTH CREEK, ZION NATIONAL PARK.

RIGHT: SANDSTONE SLOT OF WHITE CANYON.

FOLLOWING PAGES: A JANUARY GLIMPSE OF SIPAPU BRIDGE IN NATURAL BRIDGES NATIONAL MONUMENT.

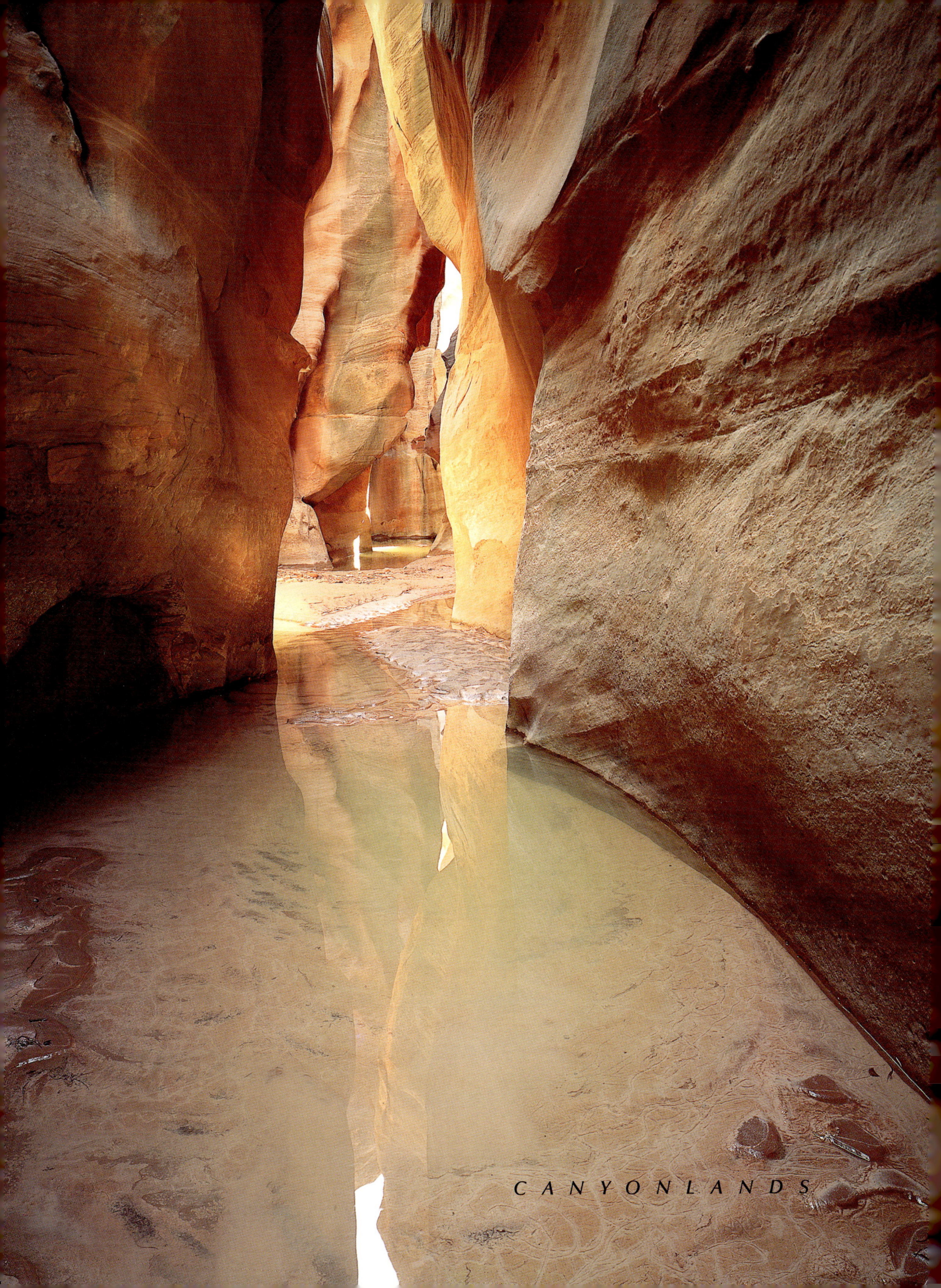

CANYONLANDS

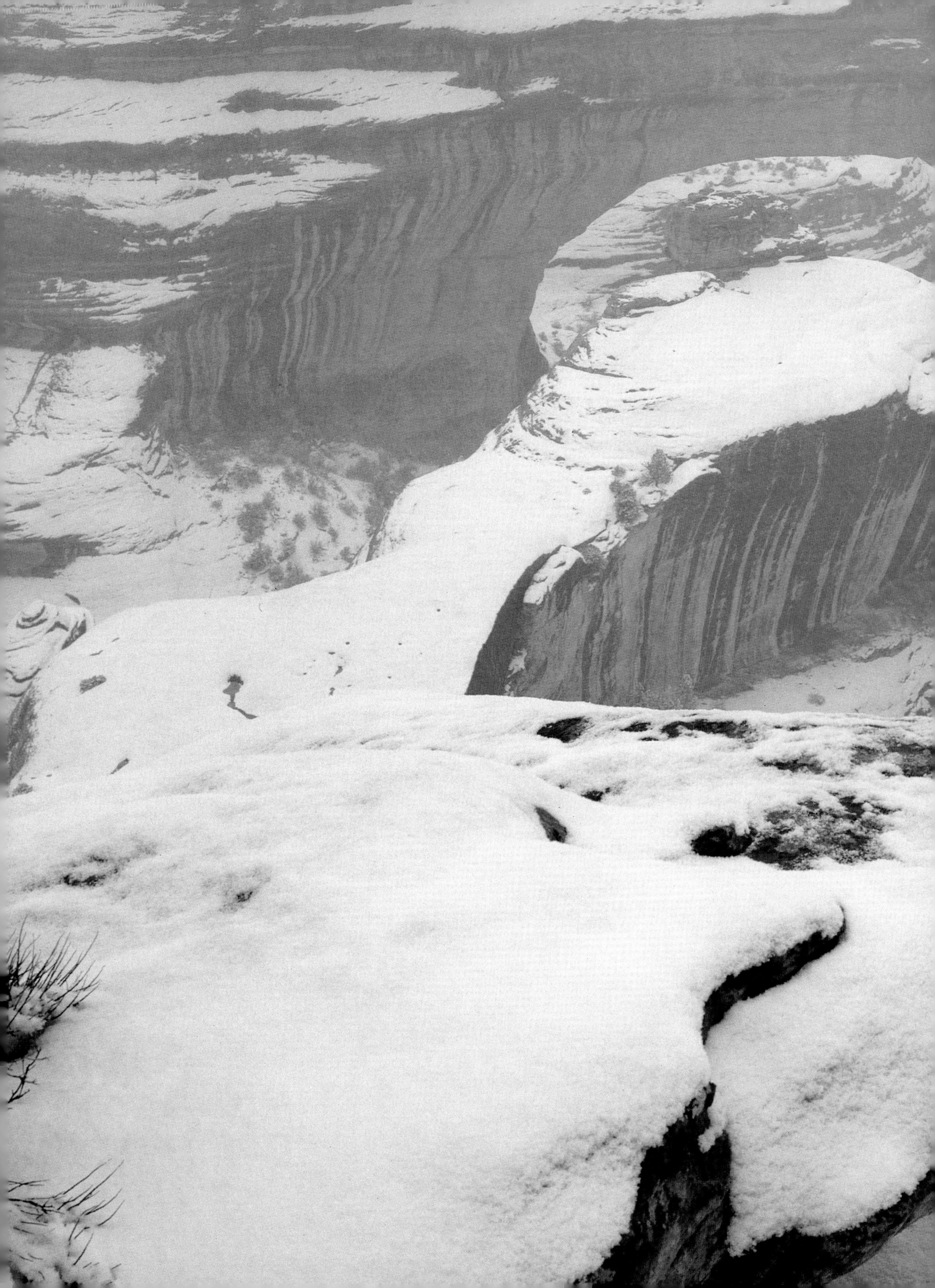

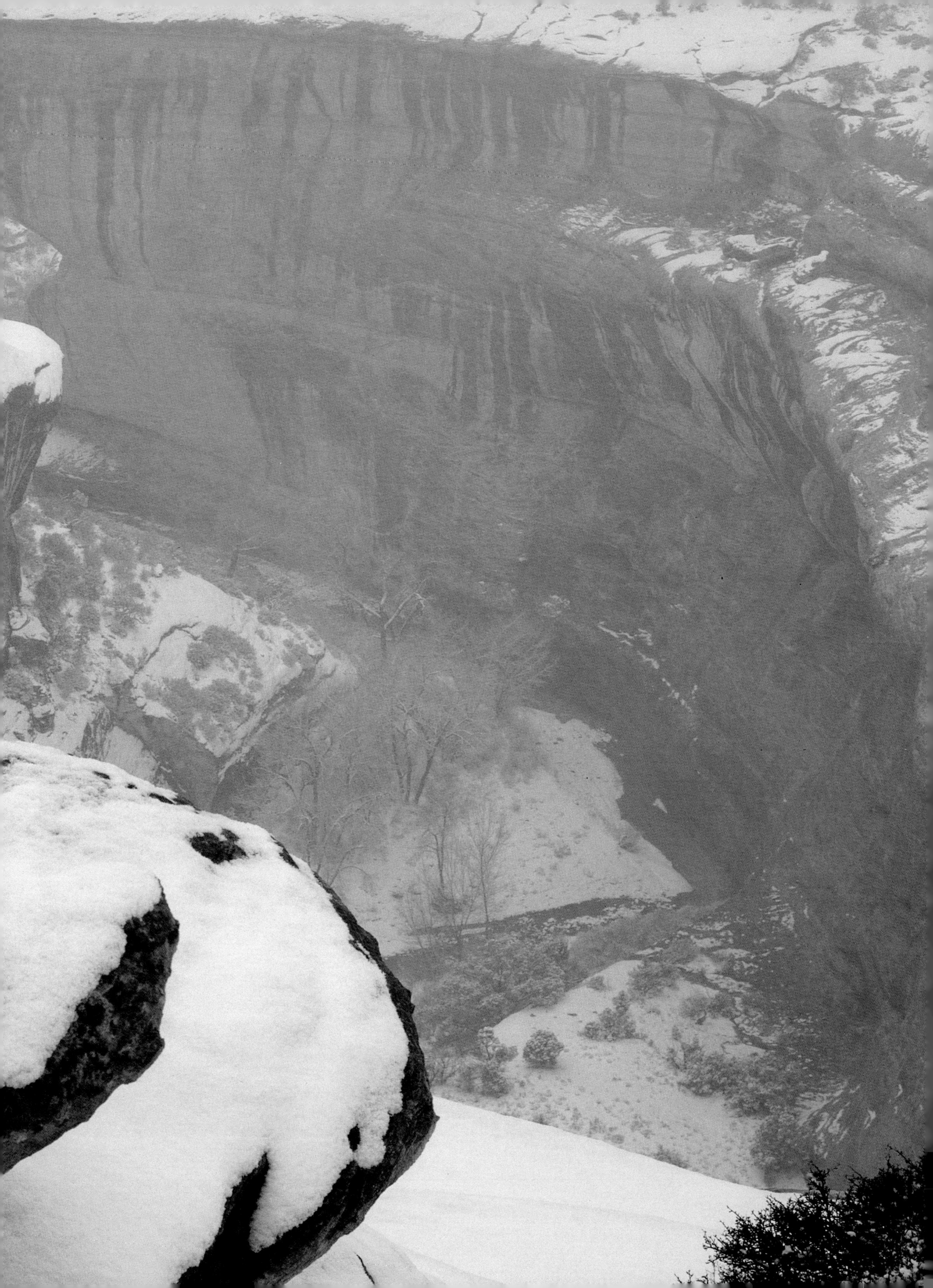

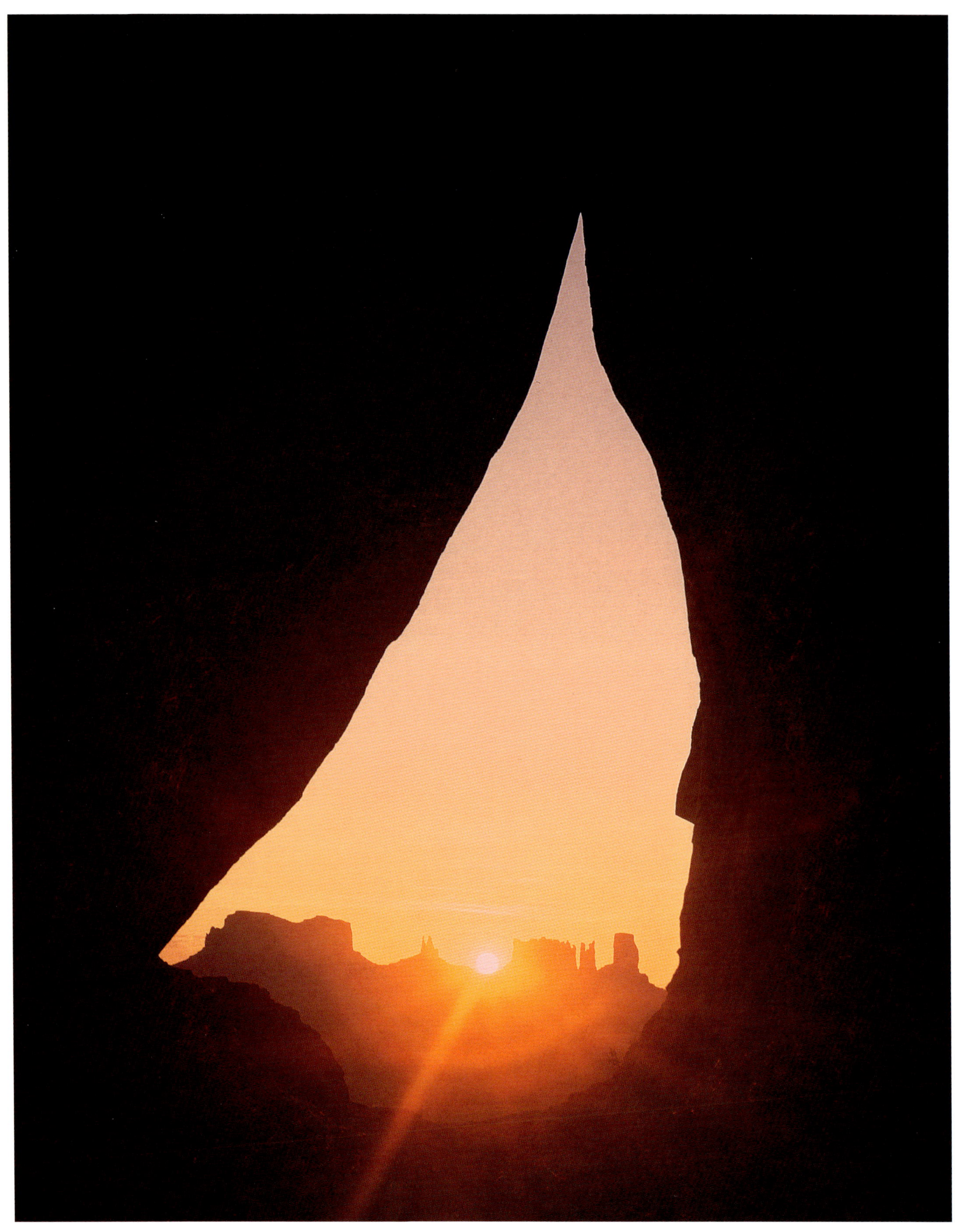

ABOVE: SANDSTONE WINDOW, MONUMENT VALLEY, NAVAJO TRIBAL PARK. *RIGHT:* STORM OVER DELICATE ARCH, ARCHES NATIONAL PARK.

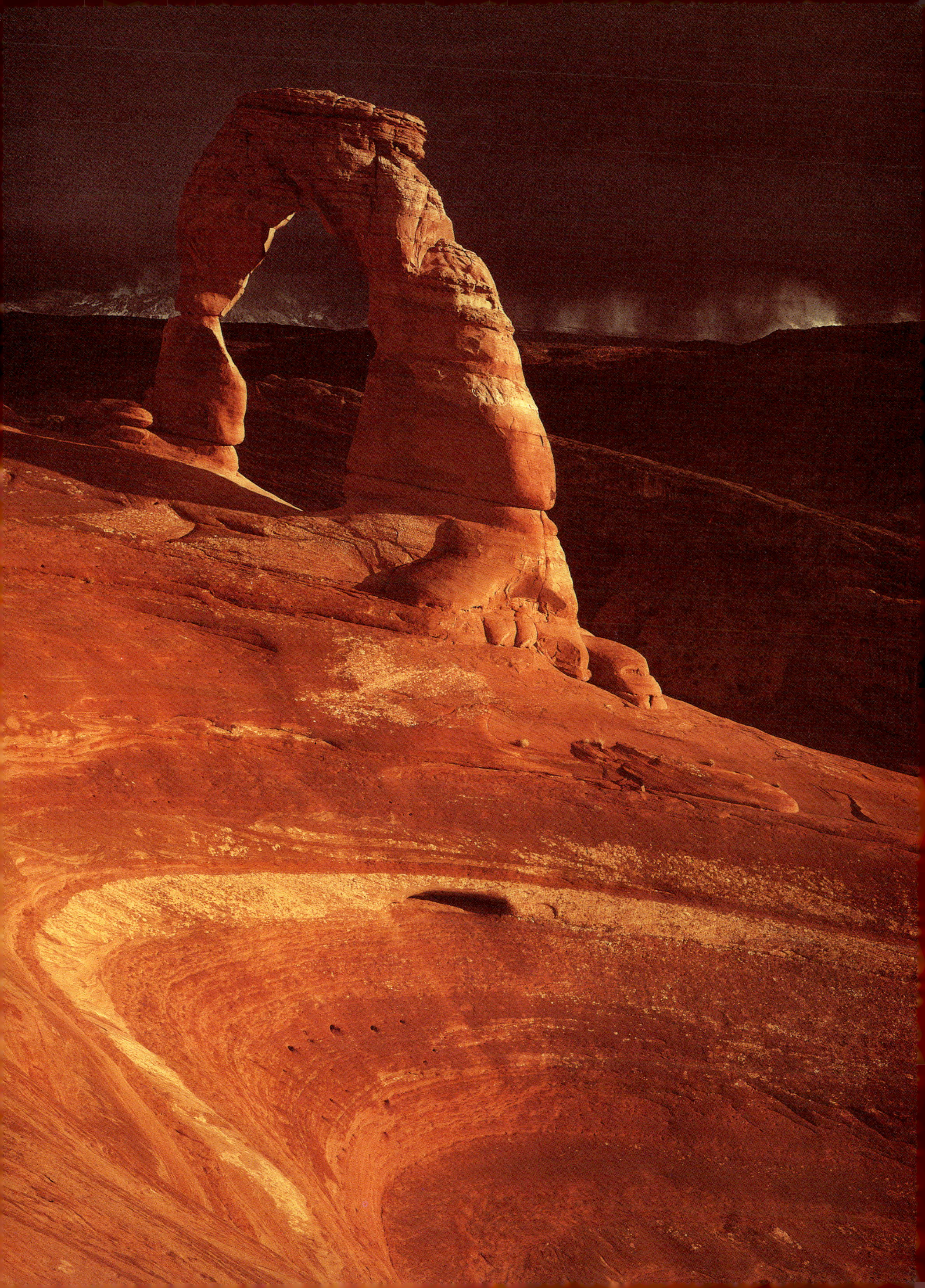

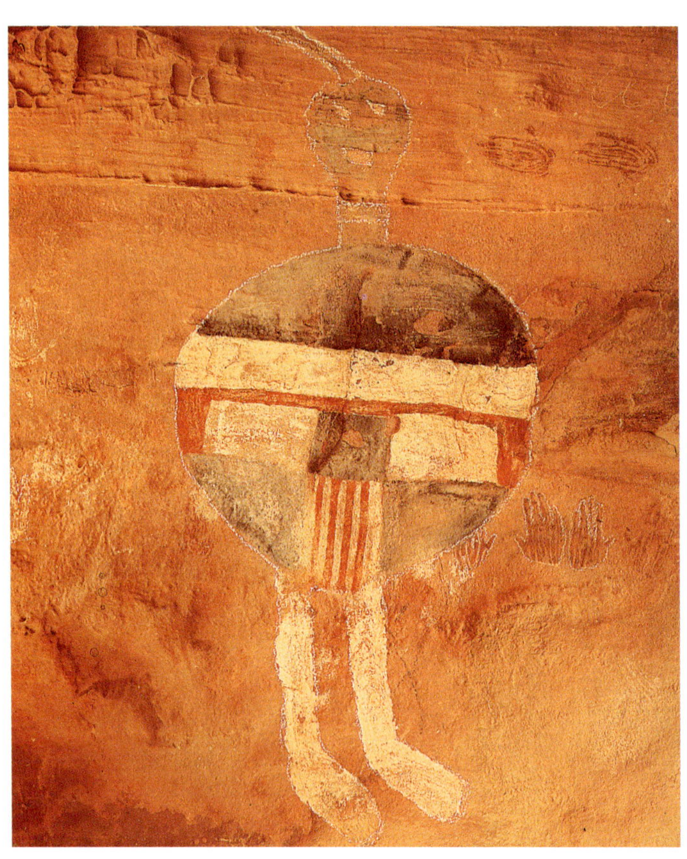

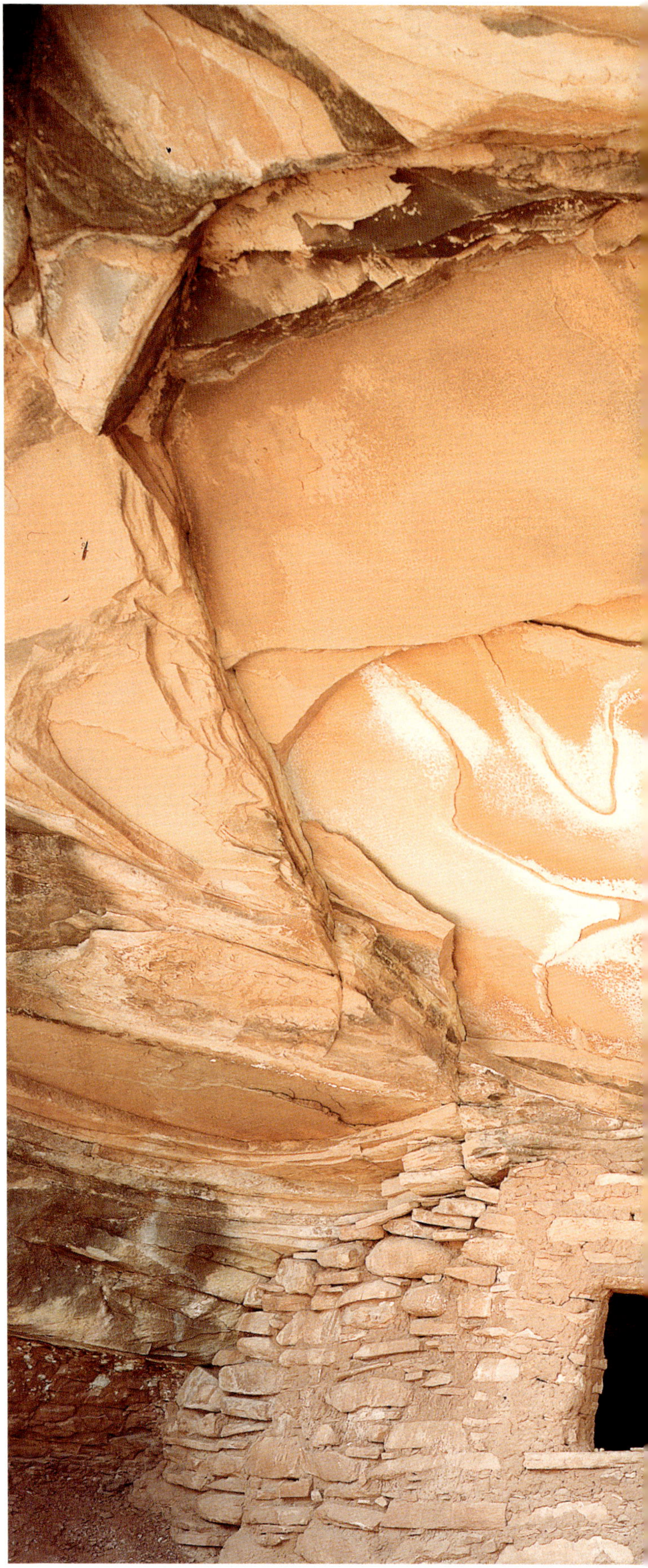

ABOVE: ANASAZI PICTOGRAPH CALLED THE ALL-AMERICAN MAN, SALT CREEK CANYON, CANYONLANDS NATIONAL PARK. *RIGHT:* ANASAZI DWELLING, CEDAR MESA.

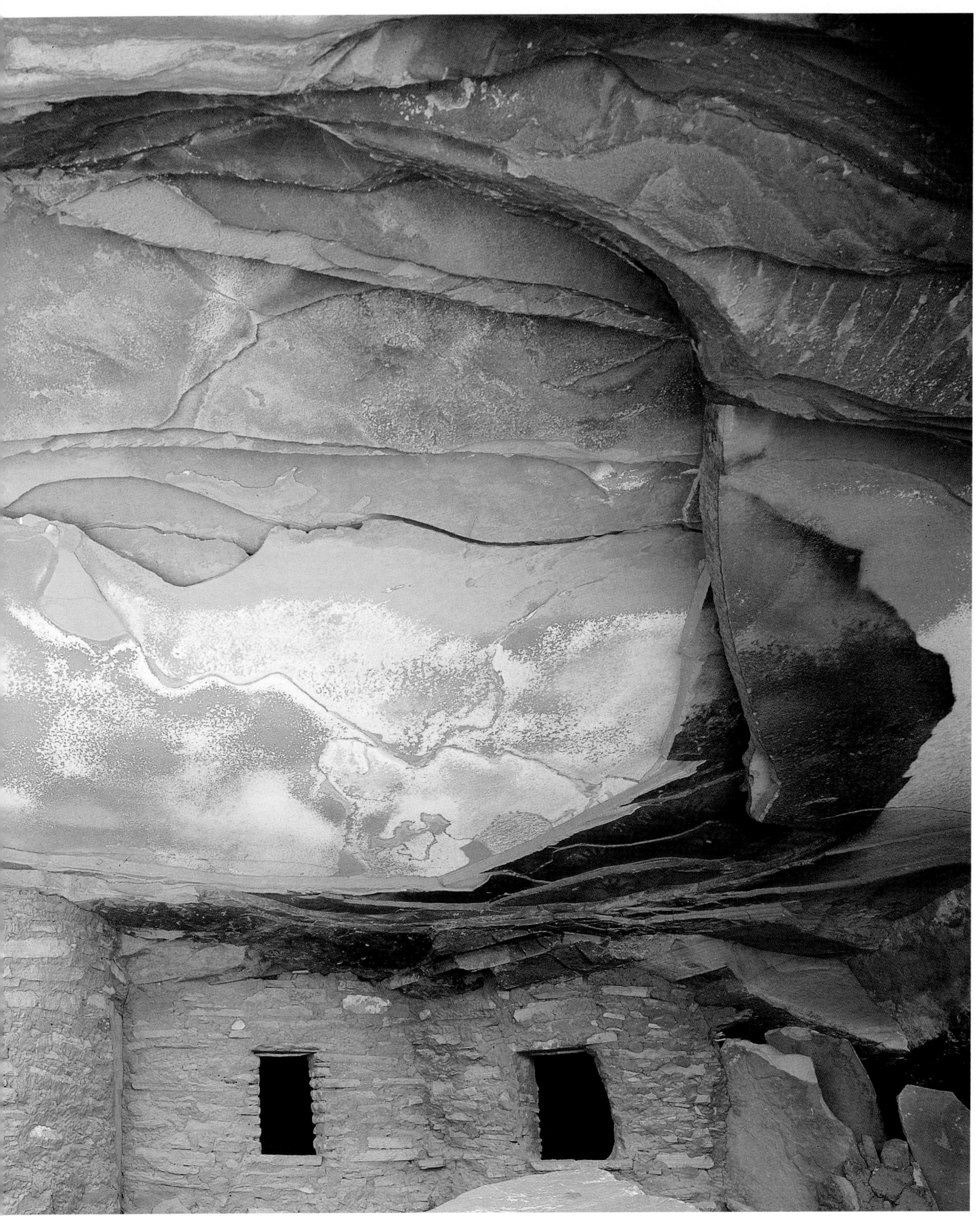

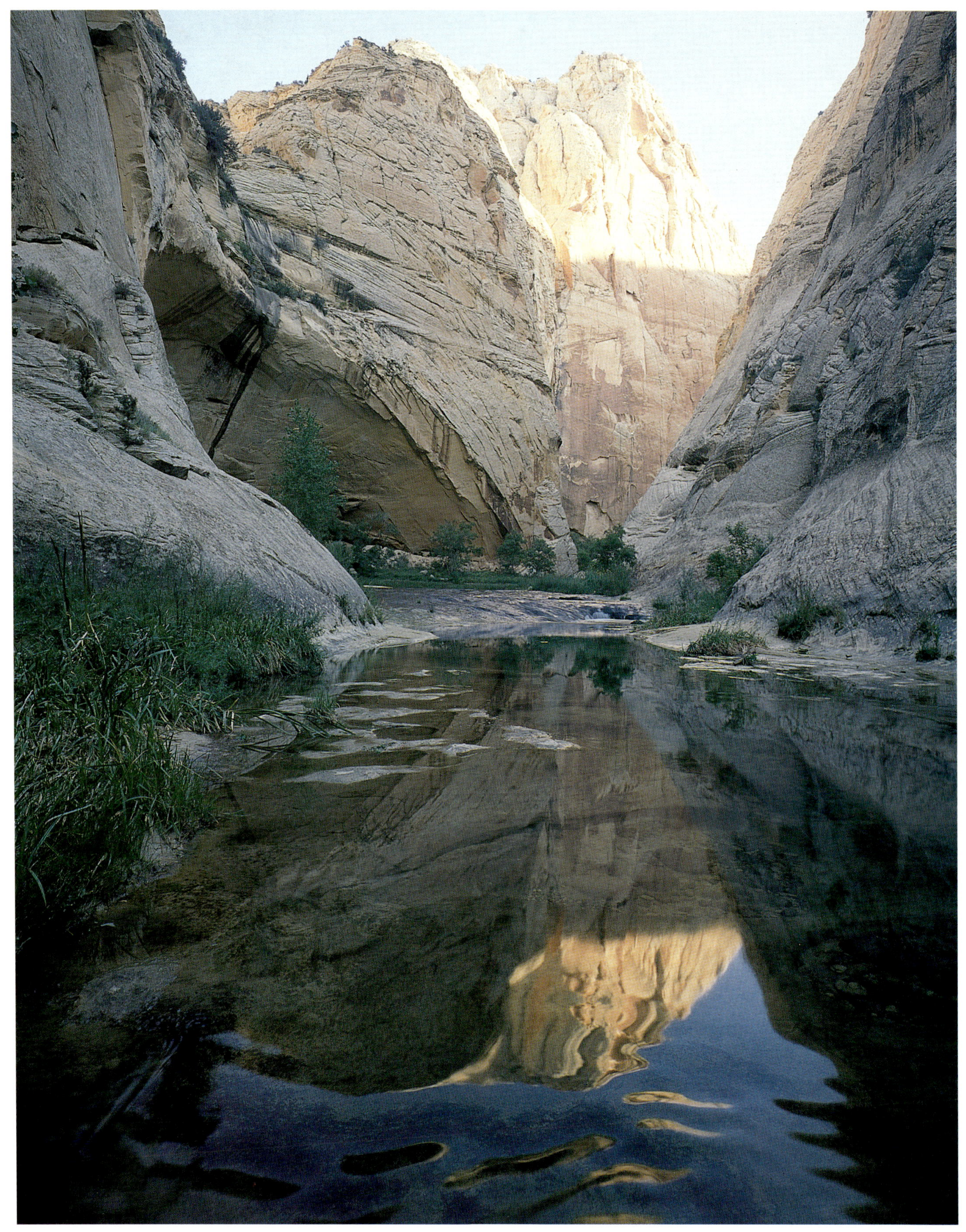

DEATH HOLLOW, GRAND STAIRCASE/ESCALANTE NATIONAL MONUMENT.

Notes between the Winds

Below the plane, a great salmon-red arch pops up like a jack-in-the-box insert in a children's book. I have never known the name of this particular arch, large enough to see from the air at two hundred miles an hour, or even precisely where it is located. Still, its delicacy always enchants me, the way it shifts in the passing light, how its shadow wreathes and defines it, and how it appears as if by magic, newly risen up each time I see it. The massive Entrada sandstone from which it is formed spalls off in huge chunks, leaving fins of rock in which erosion opens windows, eventually enlarging them to arches. This is mideastern Utah, and so many arches occur in this area that it is set aside as Arches National Park.

With this landmark arch, this carpetbagger knows she is back in a state that gathers a massive amount of splendor in a single notched rectangle—intrusions of granite that form mountains going east and west and levered-up layers that form mountains going north and south; windswept and wind-conceived sandstones from last millennium's desert and today's sandy, salty, seamless desert; sloping cliffs of finely layered red shale, ripple-marked and crumbling into greasy, treacherous talus, and sandstone cliffs of evocative hues, off-white of bone and hematite red of blood; and everything cut through by rivers that open up the layers of eternity.

None of this landscape, below or beyond, is ever one pure color; the surface is always scoured, allowing other colors to bleed through, ever-shifting, ever-changing, like layers of a San Blas embroidery cut through to reveal other colors beneath. Sometimes the terrain is velvety and puckered, sometimes patted flat and fingered smooth, more often heaped with rocks, cleft with cliffs, eroded into fanciful patterns for photographers to immortalize. I wonder, if you took southern Utah and filled the canyons with the ridges, would you come out flat and even? But then it wouldn't be the Utah I know, worked with a master craftsman's gouge, the shavings curling up along the blade edge and piling up in rims and ridges, mesas and cuestas, and magnificent mountains.

This early June morning I fly with my husband, Herman, from our home in Colorado Springs to our yearly trip with Patrick and Susan Conley down the San Juan River. Patrick and Susan believe a river trip is a wonderful opportunity to learn about the Southwest and usually run their trips with a consultant who knows a little and cares a lot about the country. As such, I've been coming back every spring for almost a dozen years, like Wendy in Peter Pan, to spring-clean the canyons, neaten up the rabbit brush, sweep the beaches, and sew the pinecone galls back on the willows.

Below, the land flattens out, spreading dry and tan. At times, the terrain is frosted gray green with big sagebrush; at other times, studded with raw umber and salmon outcrops in the subtlety of semidesert. Oftentimes a vagrant watercourse barely catches the light as it slithers through the landscape.

Ahead, the flanks of the La Sal Mountains lie green-hazed where last week's rain breathed verdure upon the clustered peaks. I remember driving Geyser Pass last fall, a pass to the north that separates two massifs of the mountains and runs beneath Haystack Peak. The peak rose like a perfect cone, streaming with rock glaciers, aproned with aspen. Seeing that place now from the air brings to mind that, for me, Utah is a complex of richly overlaid views: recalling what is on the ground from the air; and on the ground, remembering how the tiny flower at my feet fits into the all-encompassing, four-dimensional memory of sky, landform, and the time it takes to walk to nightfall.

As we lose altitude, flaps whine down, propellers change pitch, details take on definition, trees separate, and shadows refine. For a moment, I see what the raven sees, and then I am bound again to earth.

A dozen orange Sportyaks in the process of being rigged nestle neatly on the beach of Sand Island, just west of the settlement of Bluff. Before lashing in my black waterproof river bag, I drop my watch inside, shifting over to river time and obliterating the tyranny of a watch face that tells me things I don't need to know.

A Sportyak, ideal for running white water, is a sturdy, double-shelled plastic dinghy fitted with oarlocks for two six-foot oars. The rower sits directly on the bottom (no one ever uses nautical terms like deck or port or starboard with a Sportyak, or ever calls a Sportyak "she"). Sitting below the waterline puts the center of gravity low, so that the boat is both stable and maneuverable, even when awash waist-deep with water.

The advantage of a Sportyak is that you run the river yourself. No one else reads the river for you, no one else's oars push you through, no one else intercedes between you and the responsibility for staying upright. This concentration on how the river runs not only heightens awareness of all that is going on in the surrounding river world but, as one goes downstream, expands awareness to encompass a small blue planet twirling though space.

The minute I shove off from the beach, the San Juan picks up the bow and spins me out into midstream. The world breezes open as suddenly as walking from a dark room into the sunshine. I chuckle with a surge of elation, that "God's-in-his-heaven, all's-right-with-the-world" euphoria, and wonder what Robert Browning, acclimated to the closeted world of England, would think of this big, blowing, blowzy, endless-sky world of southeastern Utah. Or, for that matter, accustomed to his delicate, languid Elizabeth, think of this woman in reputably old river clothes, surrounded by waterproof bags and bailing bucket, trailing a water bottle in the river—scarcely the accoutrements of a proper Victorian lady.

Little waves peak and shimmer, patting the hull with delicious smacking sounds. Sunlight bounces off the ripples, slotting them with mauve on the downstream side, shooting dazzling flashes of light on the upstream. At the edge of an eddy, the river swirls and boils, musing to itself in hypnotic circles of thought.

The river runs around 9,000 cubic feet per second this morning, on the high side for the San Juan. To conceptualize a cubic foot per second, or cfs, visualize a tiny stream, a foot wide and a foot deep, and a foot of water on a side passing that point every second. Widen, extrapolate, envision—and 9,000 cfs becomes a very respectable amount of water. Generally at this time of year, when a lot of water is taken out for irrigation above, the San Juan runs between 1,000 and 3,000 cfs. Before Navajo Dam was built upstream, the variations in flow were extreme—anywhere from 40 cfs to 24,800 cfs—within a single year. Such flow today means that we will make good time and have fast rapids with most of their dragon's teeth well covered.

The river spins through its mile-wide valley, running a lovely *café au lait*, the common denominator color of all the mountains, all the cliffs in its landscape, all the hillsides, all the banks it pulls into itself as it comes downstream: buff, beige, chalky white, rose, burnt sienna, burnt umber, all the leftovers on a watercolorist's mixing pan swashed together in a color that unifies and pleases. The San Juan carries almost as much silt as it does water, and every slosh of water dries to a little drift of pink powder at the bottom of the boat—my San Juan River wardrobe is stained a permanent, watered-down rose.

The river is full of islands around which the current shoots. Left behind from higher flows, debris knots the branches of tamarisk and willow. The teardrop-shaped islands draw out into cobble bars on the downstream end, over which the water twinkles and gabbles, a heavenly sound like angels chattering.

Half a mile downstream, a massive cliff of Navajo sandstone forces the river into a hairpin turn to the right. I remember this wall with such vividness because it is a curve so uncluttered, so beautifully simple—a soft salmon bannered with stripes of rosy beige, tan, charcoal, or brown, washed out of the earth above, curving with the cliff's lean over the river. Sometimes vertical red lines frizzle and fray along the edges, a Navajo rug in the weaving. Sometimes darker stripes of desert varnish, that amazing mixture of minerals and heat and bacteria so prominent on desert cliffs, drizzle pennants that look tattered and shredded by the wind.

Around 245 million years ago, the Pacific coastline swung diagonally through central Utah, southwest to northeast. As the ancient sea withdrew westward to become the Pacific we know today, it added eight hundred miles to the continent and uncovered miles of sediment that have not been covered by water since. Between 200 million and 140 million years ago, this area dried to desert. Huge amounts of windblown sands blanketed most of central and western Utah, indurating to the monumental formations that make up some of the state's most spectacular scenery: the Wingate and Navajo sandstones. In places, the almost pure quartz sands of the Navajo sandstone cemented into rock up to two thousand feet thick.

The winds blowing across the deserts came out of the west and northwest. Variations in the winds' direction created large-scale crossbedding that is now bared by erosion as it slices into the fossil dune, revealing swooping, curving diagonals, a pattern as definite and as delicate as that made by sweeping a feather through wet paint. Dunes today are laid the same way, and, when some future stream cuts through them, they too will reveal these elegantly elliptical layers, formed in an eternal rhetoric of wind.

But wall-watching has its price. The usable channel, despite the river's width, is shallow and narrow. The fast current on the outside of the curve tends to shoot a boat directly into the wall, scoop it up and flip it unceremoniously. Staying farther out in the river offers little improvement: sandbars weave just under the surface of the opaque water, and the boat plows into one with a hearty thunk. Wedging hard into a sandbar means disembarking, pushing off and grabbing your boat before

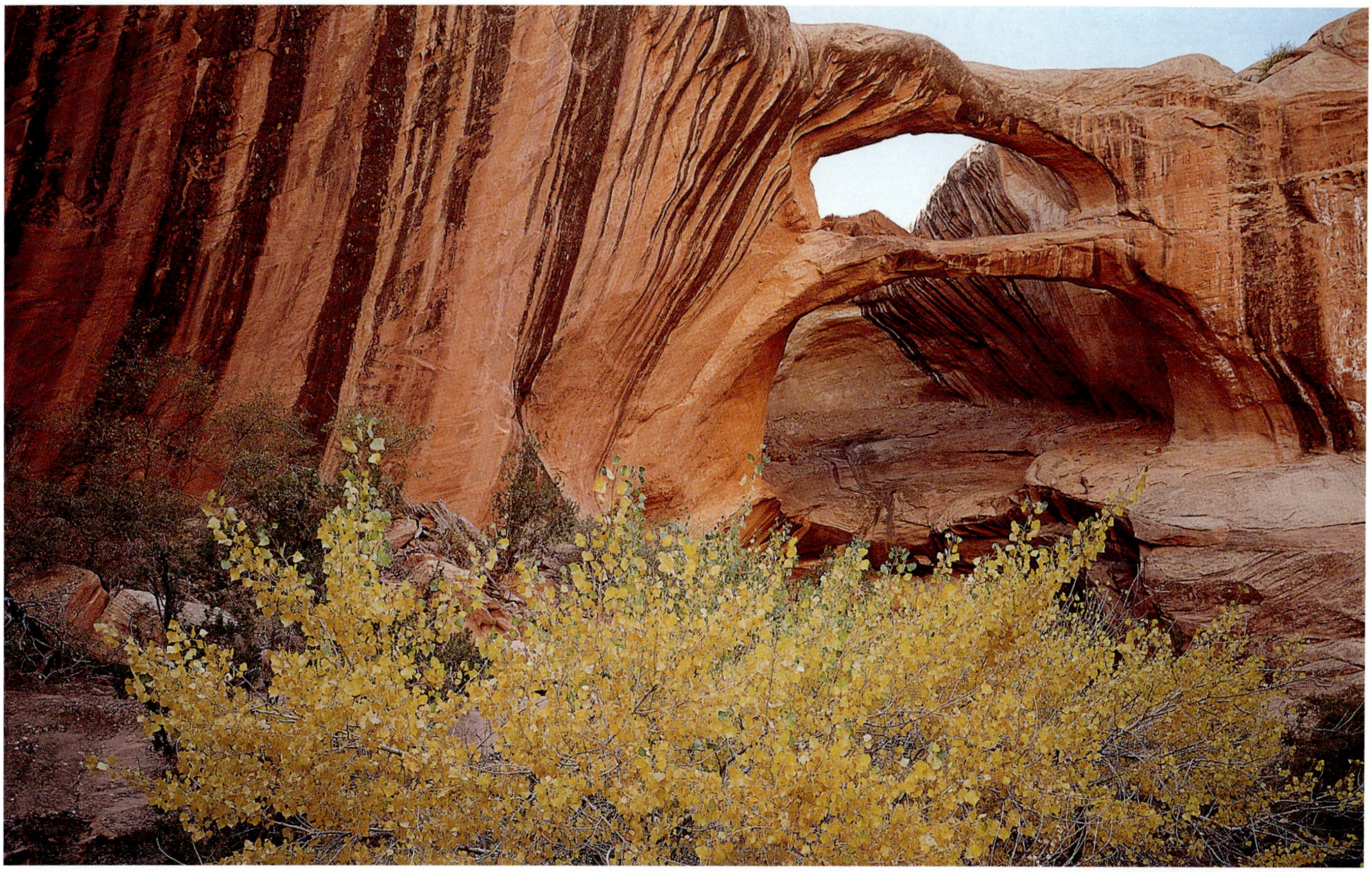

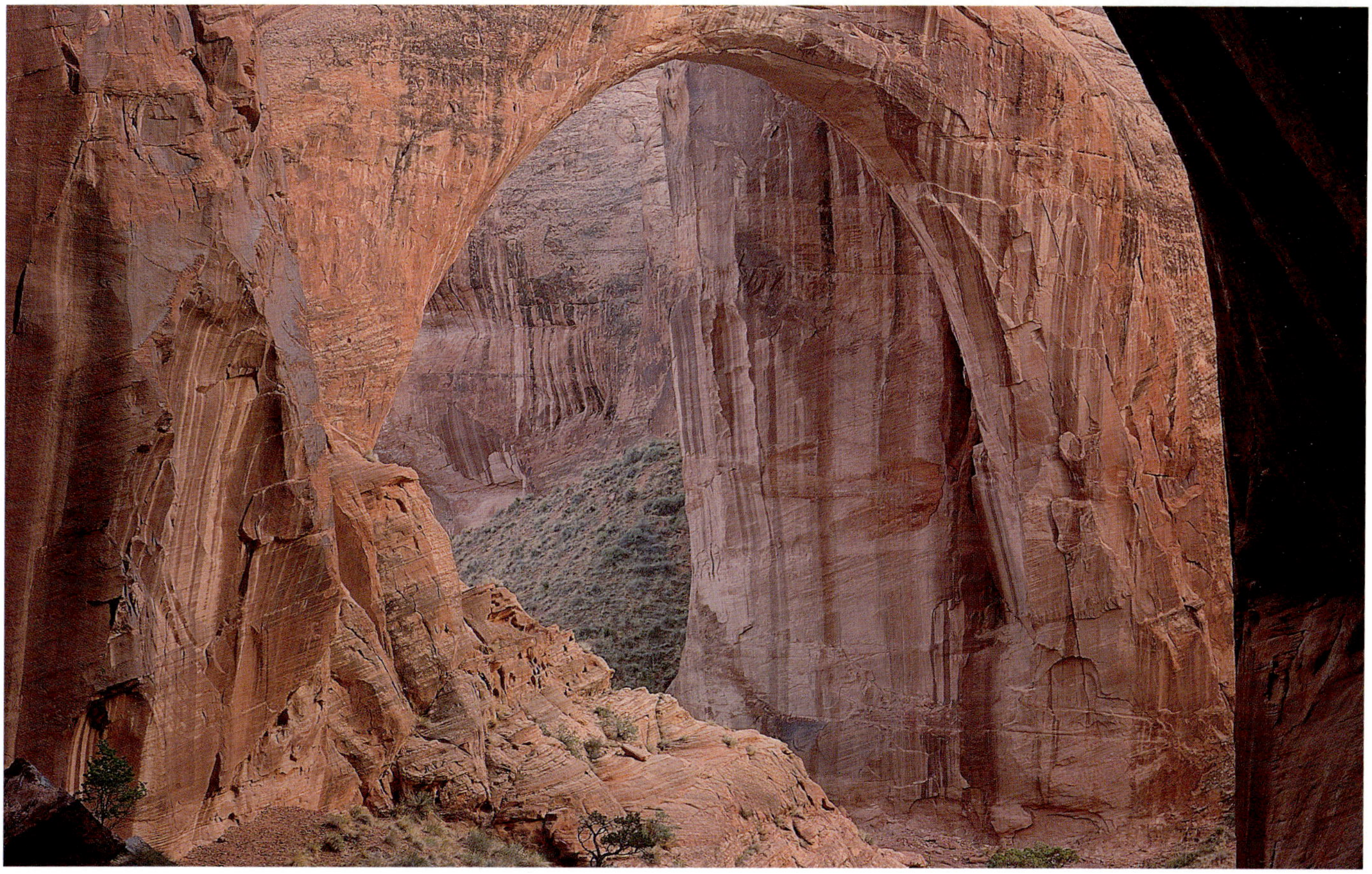

TOP: BRIMHALL ARCH, COTTONWOOD, CAPITOL REEF NATIONAL PARK. *BOTTOM:* RAINBOW BRIDGE, RAINBOW BRIDGE NATIONAL MONUMENT.

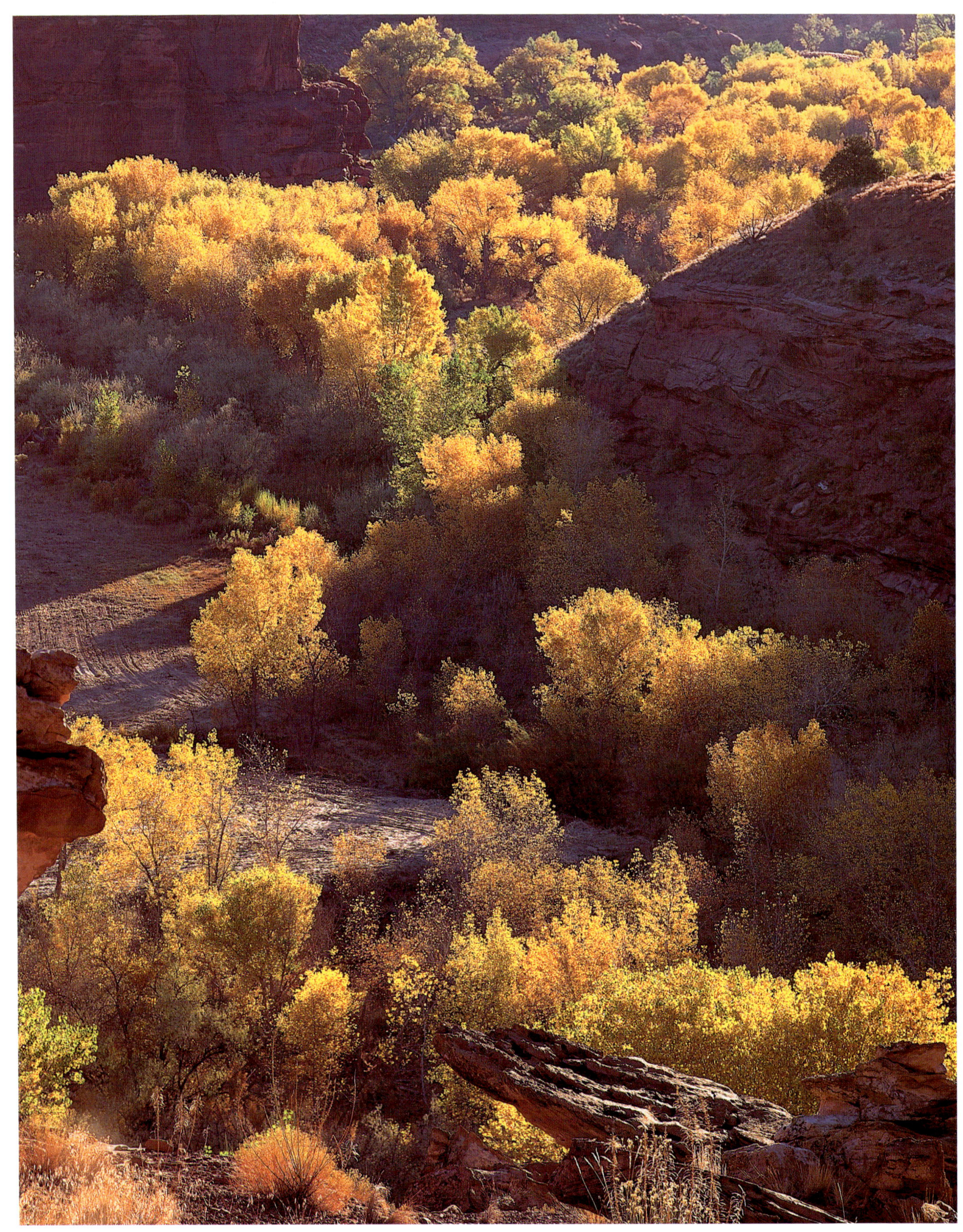

AUTUMN, ESCALANTE RIVER, GRAND STAIRCASE/ESCALANTE NATIONAL MONUMENT.

it gets out of arm's reach, lunging back in, and suffering the ignominy of it all.

Seven miles downstream, Mormon settlers, in the winter of 1879-80, ascended a steep, narrow slot in the sandstone from the river to the uplands above. Two hundred men and women, fifty children, more than a hundred teams, and almost as many wagons, had been sent on a mission from St. George in southern Utah to establish a colony to the east near Montezuma Creek. They crossed the Colorado at Hole-in-the-Rock, came across Clay Hills Pass, looped around the head of Grand Gulch, and then, thwarted by the huge, high wall of Comb Ridge, were forced down to the San Juan River. When they reached the river, they turned up these sandstone steps to gain the open land eastward.

To traverse the same path, we hike across a high, open terrace semé with smooth, rounded river cobbles. Each rests on its own pedestal of dirt, a pedestal decades in the forming as wind winnowed away the loose soil around it. The river, now a hundred feet below and a quarter mile away, knocked these stones together as efficiently as a lapidary tumbler, polished them with silt, and left them to the warmth of the suns of centuries. In this heated-up silence, one fits in my hand like comfort.

Then the ascent the Mormons made over one hundred years ago begins. I trudge upward across the slabbed and swirled ledges of Navajo sandstone, looking for fragments of the dugway the Mormons built; to facilitate the climb they piled rocks to form a more or less even surface. The dugway is not easy to see, for the Navajo sandstone itself is irregular, rounded, and hummocky, and so friable that it breaks down into loose fragments that lodge in every crevice. The faces of quartz crystals in the sandstone glitter in the sun. Only twigs of plants, separate and wide-spaced, have footholds here: blackbrush, rice grass, Mormon tea, matchweed. Lichens scab the sandstone—pale gray, dark brown, black, dirty yellow, ocher—flaking off as the rock exfoliates, holding the sand grains in their short, tough rhizomes.

Up this unbelievable slot of crumbling rock, up an incline so steep it is beyond the most macho four-wheeler, the Mormons dragged and pulled and coaxed and cajoled and whipped their oxen. So terrible was the effort that in speaking of it years later, grown men broke into tears.

The settlement, which they called Bluff, was abandoned after a few years: the original information about the area was faulty; too many Indians looked in the windows at unexpected times while the men were in the fields; the hard, dry, salty ground was impossible to farm without irrigation, and it was impossible to dig irrigation works with so few people; there was too much silt in the river water to drink or be settled out with cottonwood ashes; they had the usual sicknesses. In a few years, the Mormon Church relented and allowed them to move on, north to Blanding or Monticello, or home to St. George.

At the tip of the sandstone slope, it is just a short scramble to a view that looks across an intervening wash to Comb Ridge itself. The panoply of exposed rock stands as if on an easel, pushed up at a forty-five-degree angle in great panels of stone—a brilliantly colored, strikingly formed façade of dusky purple reds, creamy whites, and russets, layers of hardened sediments, raised and eroded into great, galloping sculptural shapes.

Much of the stunning scenery in Utah occurs in the swells and upwarps that crack open with dramatic juxtapositions of blatant color and thrusting rock. Comb Ridge marks the eastern boundary of the huge Monument Upward, an asymmetrical fold of earth forty to sixty miles wide, which crosses southeastern Utah, runs north and south of the San Juan for a hundred miles, and through which the river cuts.

Only the skyline of Comb Ridge is straight, a rusty red wall meeting a brilliant blue morning sky. Two sandstones combine to form a cliff over three hundred feet high, a thin layer of Kayenta sandstone toppling and transitioning into Wingate sandstone with no visible break. Wingate sandstone is actually off-white on fresh fracture, but turns ruddy when the iron oxide it contains is exposed to air. Beneath it are the eye-catching, multicolored Chinle formations whose ancient stream channels flowed here some 200 million years ago. Today, the Chinle is known for containing large amounts of petrified wood and uranium. Long lenses of unlikely colors—peach, gray green, lavender, yellow green, and pink, as well as rusty tans and browns—stripe its rounded slopes. Finally, at the base, great scallops of white Navajo sandstone ballast the ridge, as in many other upwarps in Utah.

Far below, the river curves into coolness, and the fine, soaring green of cottonwoods whispers shade.

The great, rollicking rollers called sand waves are not unique to the San Juan, but they are unusually well developed in this reach of the river. Special conditions of flow and bed spawn them, along with sufficient velocity and a plenitude of silt. When water flows over a sandy or silty bottom, it creates asymmetrical ripples, trending downstream. When velocity increases, the swifter current flattens the ripples, and the bottom smoothes out and simmers with sand. With greater increase in velocity, anti-dunes form, larger but unstable ripples of sand building upstream. The surface waves reflect this and likewise build and break upstream, big lolloping waves that the boat rides like a roller coaster.

By midafternoon, clouds build quickly to the west. Thunder grumbles. We pull off-river early. I try to pitch my tent. Gusts of wind pick up everything not tied down. With a stake in half-way, the tent threatens to take off, flapping like a wild sail set loose on a universe not of its own making. I unfold my rain jacket as the first squall hits. The rain comes, stinging and horizontal and cold. Out here, one does not escape the vagaries of nature by virtue of man's roofs and umbrellas. In a desert rainstorm, woman is just another wet, bedraggled part of nature.

After a windy night, morning opens calm, cool, and fresh. I stand on an apron of damp sand at the water's edge and brush my teeth, feeling unreasonably good about life in general. Accidentally, I dislodge a piece of wood half buried in the sand. Beneath it prowls a formidable critter about three inches long, a large larva near its last instar, for it has wing pads and a head with pincer jaws that look as if they could take a finger off. It is a hellgrammite, the aquatic larva of a dobsonfly. Adult dobsonflies resemble large damselflies but carry into adult-hood these malevolent mandibles. In the slight depression left by the log are four more holes in a row with four more hellgrammites, in various stages of maturity, writhing in the unwelcome light.

For the moment, I am where I most want to be, brushing my teeth into a larking river I love, watching lavender and gold reflections shimmy downstream. I want to stretch the moment, to enjoy this morning another day longer, but I turn and walk back to camp—there's only so long one can keep brushing one's teeth.

Some 150 miles northwest of Bluff as the redtail flies, 2,000 miles from New York and 750 miles from San Francisco, a little west of Fantasy and a bit east of Incredible lies the town of Escalante. Just beyond it, heading north, is the Escalante Rim, a Roman-striped wall of elegant charcoal grays and khakis, the capping rim rolling just enough for variety, the face straight enough to maintain the integrity of the layers, unnotched and unbuttressed. If you want to keep out enemies, don't build the Great Wall of China. Build an Escalante Rim.

Some miles beyond, around a high corner, the land suddenly falls away, laying open a panorama so superlative that I have to read it, left to right, in order to comprehend it. The last time I saw this view it was painted small in the background of a Renaissance crucifixion by a fifteenth-century painter portraying a rocky Gethsemane he knew only in the fertility of his imagination. Here, massive bosses of white Navajo sandstone set off hollowed and ledged red walls; knobs and hillocks of rock—as rounded as pillows, as sheared off as shattered ice, smoothed, cajoled—form a sculpture garden for Brobdingnagians.

In the midst of this stage set, crawling out of the Waterpocket Fold, wends the Escalante River. Into it loops a small, unnamed, commonplace, garden-variety arroyo. Fifteen feet wide, the steep walls stand eight feet high so that I cannot see over when I am down inside. A thread of a stream recently serpentined back and forth, from wall to wall, leaving a line of smooth, unhurried sand. If it were not the dry season, I would not even consider walking this arroyo, for the banks rise so precipitously that there is no way I could get out should a flash flood canter down. On sober consideration, I probably shouldn't be here now—but good sense does not a naturalist make.

I justify the foolhardiness by enjoying the quiet, the sense of being cloistered, sequestered. Open to the sky, this arroyo is nevertheless as walled in as a medieval passageway. Here I am privy to root secrets and pebble thoughts, to small green plants that spread shiny rosettes in the sand, to a hedge of willows, narrow leafed and beset with rosy galls. A huge cottonwood has fallen across the streambed and almost blocks passage. Gray, disheveled, splitting, it never made peace with its demise. Its branches look as if they reached for help and nobody came; and the tree fell, clutching for air.

I scramble up the bank and find an old Utah juniper to curl up beneath. A flamboyant tree, it flings a cape of branches over its shoulder and sports a romantic broad-rimmed hat of needles and a flowing beard of bark—in short, a personage. Whatever this tree does, it does with panache. It sports three trunks—two dead, the third alive and growing at a conveniently rakish angle. When I settle in, this branch holds my backpack, a pair of wet socks, a dirty shirt; hangers my mirror; hooks my canteen strap; shelters my sleeping; and fringes my sky. All my world is within arm's reach.

This old juniper is but one of numberless gnarled and shreddy trees that circle the mountains of Utah. I remember them in the House and the Ruby Mountains, part of those "caterpillars crawling south," as an early geologist characterized the basin-and-range topography of western Utah. I recall how they wreathe the volcanic Henry Mountains. The last-named mountains in the United States, the Henrys were named after Professor Joseph Henry, the first Secretary of the Smithsonian Institute. I remember them along the Uintas, the open individuals giving way to the denser, darker growth of ponderosa pine, Douglas fir, and blue spruce. Closed-in, carbon-copy trees in closed-in forests, growing in dark and somber canyons with cool downdrafts and needle-padded ground, are the antithesis of this individualistic juniper's open, reaching grasp, demanding attention, pushing the sky around, making its presence count. Never mind those neat conical trees, prim and proper, playing tiddlywinks every Tuesday. This tree is outlandish, the profligate gambler throwing its berries like blue dice upon the ground, making its bargains with the devil and keeping an extra ace or two under its bark.

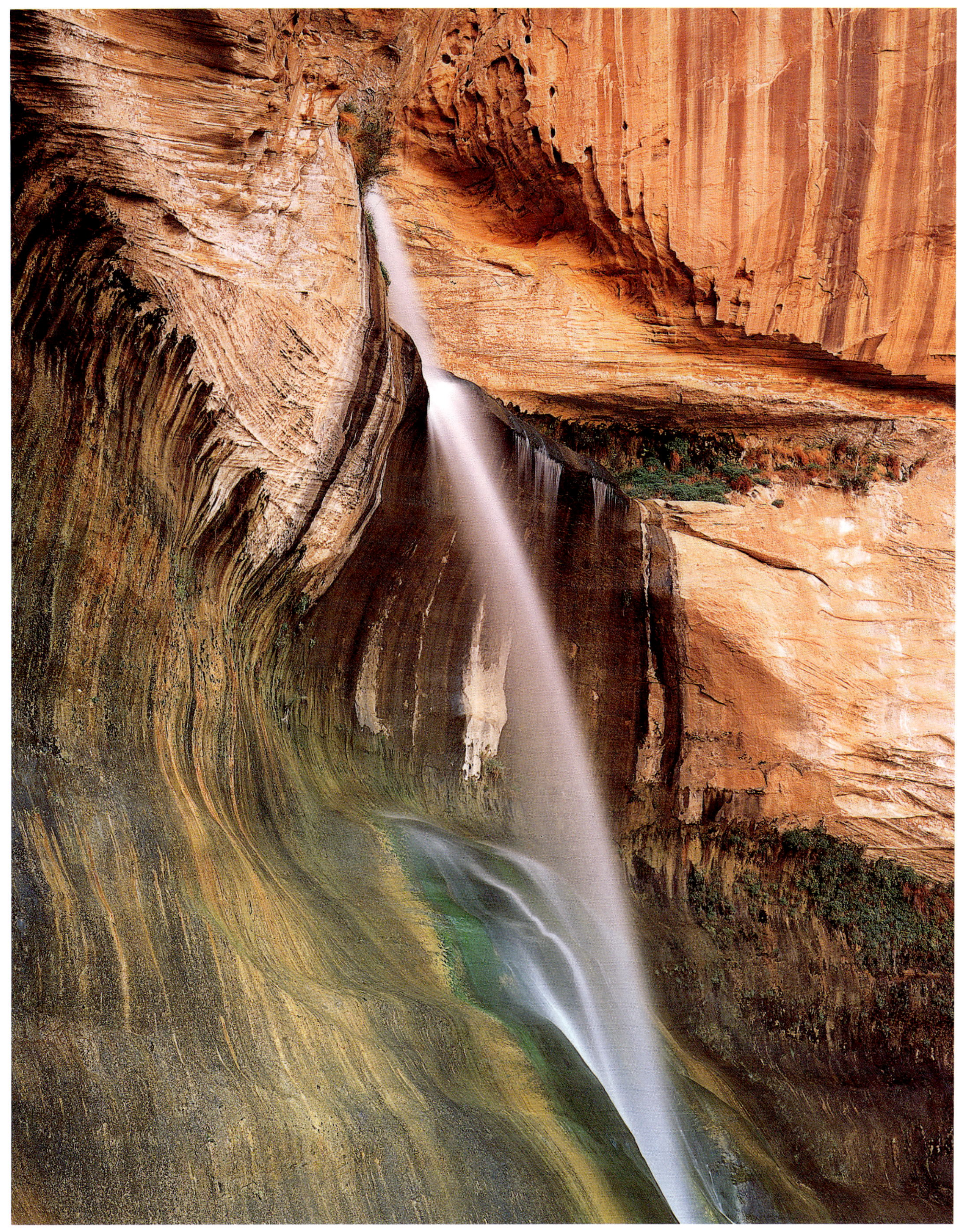

LOWER CALF CREEK FALLS, ESCALANTE CANYONS, GRAND STAIRCASE/ESCALANTE NATIONAL MONUMENT.

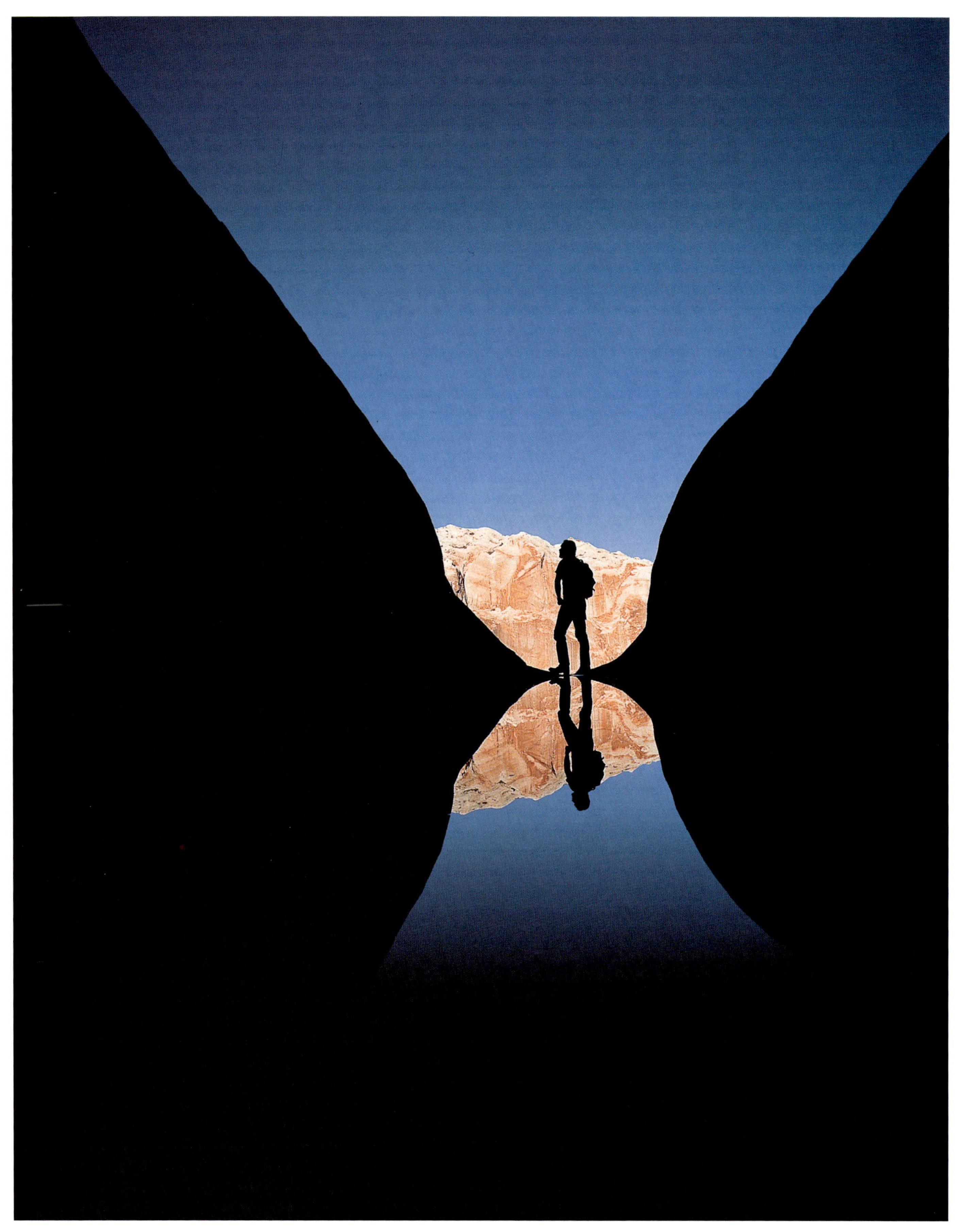

WATERPOCKET POOL REFLECTION, WATERPOCKET FOLD, CAPITOL REEF NATIONAL PARK.

I, in turn, empty my canteen at its feet when I leave. Not much, but in this land, water is the ultimate gift. This tree was here before I was and will be here when I am not, but I have the hand that writes. Before I leave, I inscribe its dusty doormat with block letters: IMMORTAL JUNIPER, MCMLXXXIX.

I turn to leave and stop. Something is missing. With a flourish, I add an extra "X" of affection and get on my way.

The Fremont River—named after John Charles Fremont, the nineteenth-century explorer who identified the interior drainage of the Great Basin—runs through a corner of Capitol Reef National Park. There it skirts a ravishing sandstone wall washed with peach tan silt that masks its true color. At its foot, huge blocks tumble over each other, deeply tinted on old faces, ivory on those more recently spalled off. In this massive progression of wall, there are all kinds of lithic experiments, as if a master sculptor had roughed out these monstrously large blocks and piled them aside, ready to work tomorrow. Already carved are Swiss cheese panels of great intricacy, a jutting simian profile, and an Easter Island head, seventy-five feet tall, that looks eastward, its features defined by sharp fractures.

Two deer at riverside, ears alert, watch me. Deciding that anyone writing in a notebook must be harmless, they continue browsing downstream, so well camouflaged that I see them only when a white rump patch moves. Rabbitbrush screens me, and overhead a big old cottonwood stretches its branches out over the water. Its dried twigs and leaves cover the ground, and I debate whether to clear a spot or leave them beneath my ground cloth and crinkle all night.

A cobble bar downstream interrupts the river, making it warble. Late sun hits the sandstone cliff full on. Across the water is a shaded sandy beach, and I think about putting on my sneakers and lugging my gear across. A fawn moves slowly behind a stand of dead cottonwood on the other side. I will not intrude. As if sensing my thoughts, the pair of deer on this side raise their heads, watch me intently, then bound across the river with neat plashes. Four more that I hadn't seen, including a buck, cross with leisure, and all of a sudden there are ten—then eleven—and even as I write, twelve more, herding up for the evening like crows.

I, too, settle in for the evening, pull on my old sweater the color of dried cottonwood leaves, and put my day to bed.

Still going northward, I catch breakfast at Hanksville and head for the San Rafael Swell. No farmer, no cattleman, could look at this Green River Desert landscape with any affection whatsoever. The aesthetics here are of the earth's bare bones revealed in juxtapositions of shape and color, not the aesthetics of productivity.

From Capitol Reef, the light picks out the pale edging of Navajo sandstone, three tiers crisp and cloud white, bays sharply drawn. These swells and uplifts and domes that pattern Utah were raised at the same time as the Rocky Mountains, but into gentle upwarps instead of high peaks. Nevertheless, the San Rafael Swell, with its color-banded walls and pinnacled profiles, is as dramatic as the most assertive mountain.

You don't have to go to a national park or monument to find wilderness in Utah. Although I pay homage to places like Arches and Bryce Canyon and Capitol Reef National Parks and to Cedar Breaks and Natural Bridges National Monuments, the places that remain most vividly in my mind are not these described and photographed and formalized parks and monuments. The places that remain in my memory belong to the outback—the places you can't get to from here, the places few people travel, the roads the car says I shouldn't be on, the places with nothing tacked on to the end of their geologic or geographic names, and even places without names.

Into the San Rafael Swell, I settle myself beneath a cliff somewhere to contemplate the quality of the ancient oceans and the wiles of water. My chosen wall is a sandy Chinook-salmon pink, paler at the bottom, a deeper, smokier hue at the top, reticulated by water into a network of fine veins. As I sketch the intricate erosion pattern, I force the pen to stutter on the page to catch the quick delicacy of the design.

I measure the wall's height by the number of handholds that it would take for me to scale it and estimate it to be over a hundred feet. Minute shrubs dot the face wherever they are able to grab a foothold, seeking out their year's quotient of water from the rare rains, and since the rain is generally smaller than that quotient, the leaves are tiny and gray and crisp; the shrubs, dwarfed. No matter. Aesthetics is not the point. Survival is.

Hand flat on rock, the antagonism between rock and plant pulses through my palm. The rock asserts sheer cliffs that shed all soil. The cliff abhors the horizontal, eschews the hospitable ledge. But the seed insinuates anyway, snakes down a hairlike root, niddles aside a few grains of rock, and sends up a green sprout. Talus and debris may bury it, but the shoot lengthens and survives, even creates another root thread or thrusts out a new leaf as defiant as a revolutionary banner.

Maybe there's something to be said for being transitory and adventitious, living for the moment, gambling on a hairline crack for root space and a drop of water for sustenance. Forget the monuments in responsible stone, upright and seemingly eternal. Give me a cell streaming protoplasm, a little sunlight, and a green smile.

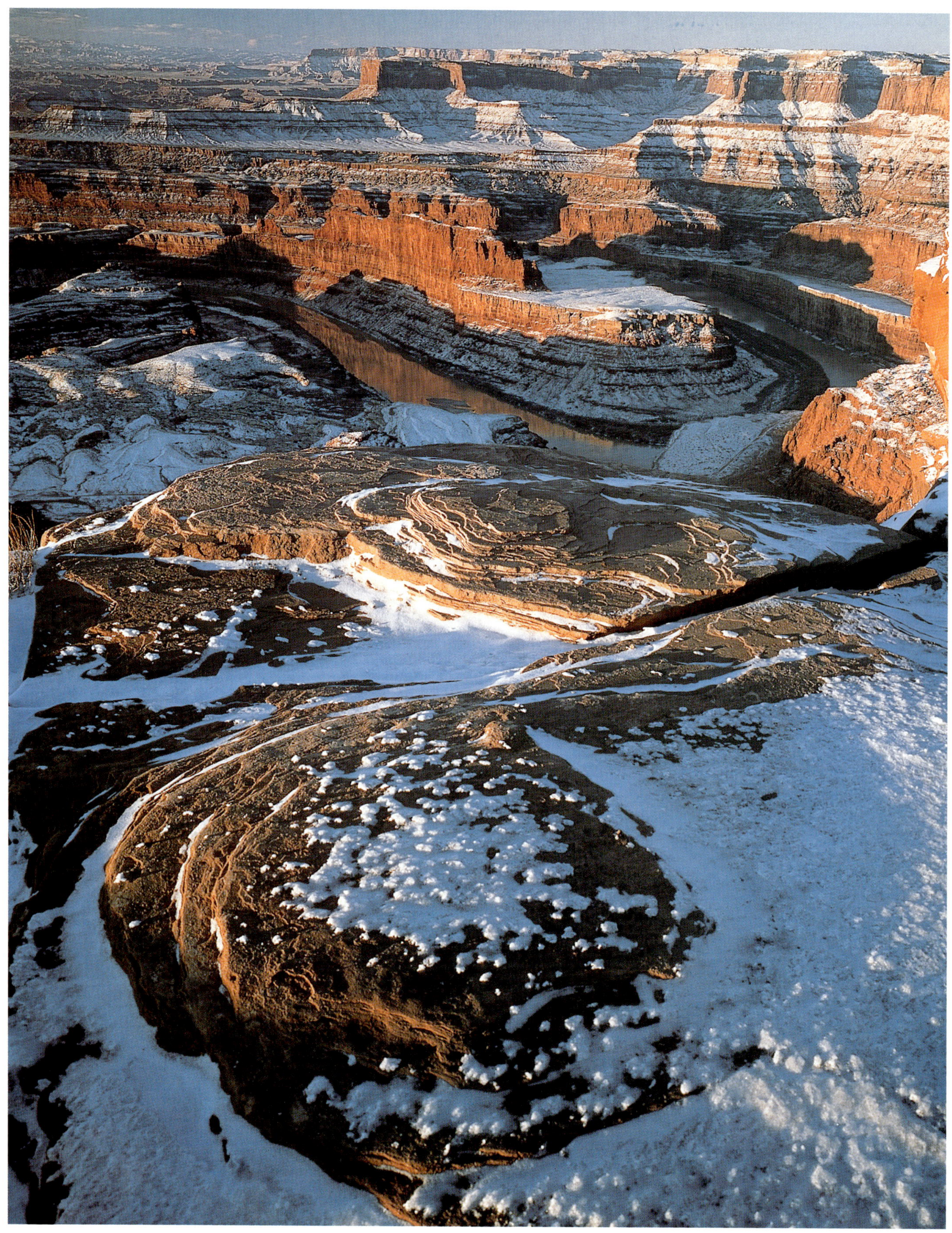

SNOWS ETCH RIMS ABOVE THE COLORADO RIVER, FROM DEADHORSE POINT STATE PARK, INCLUDES CANYONLANDS NATIONAL PARK.

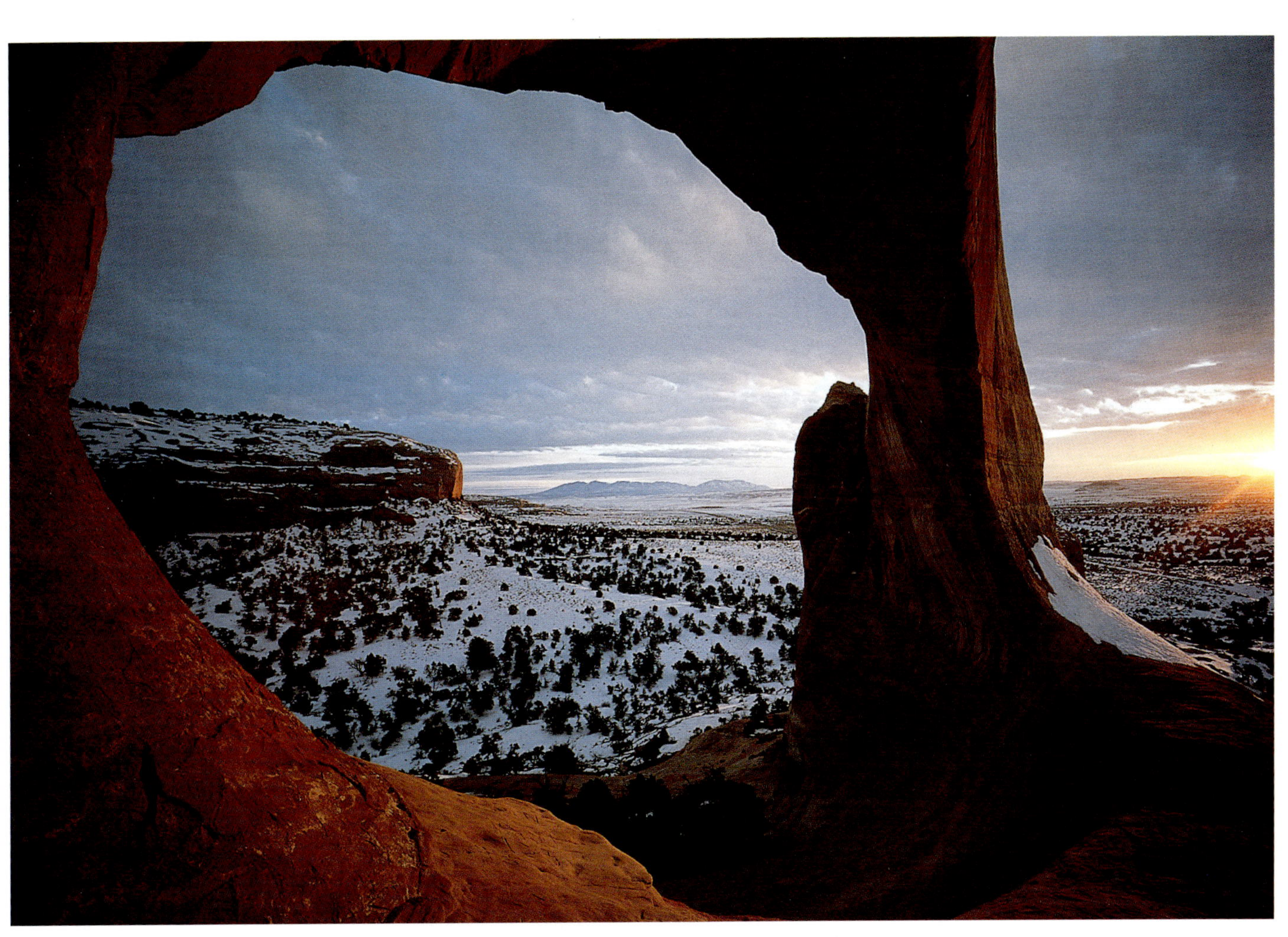

WINTER SUN, WILSON ARCH, CANYONLANDS.

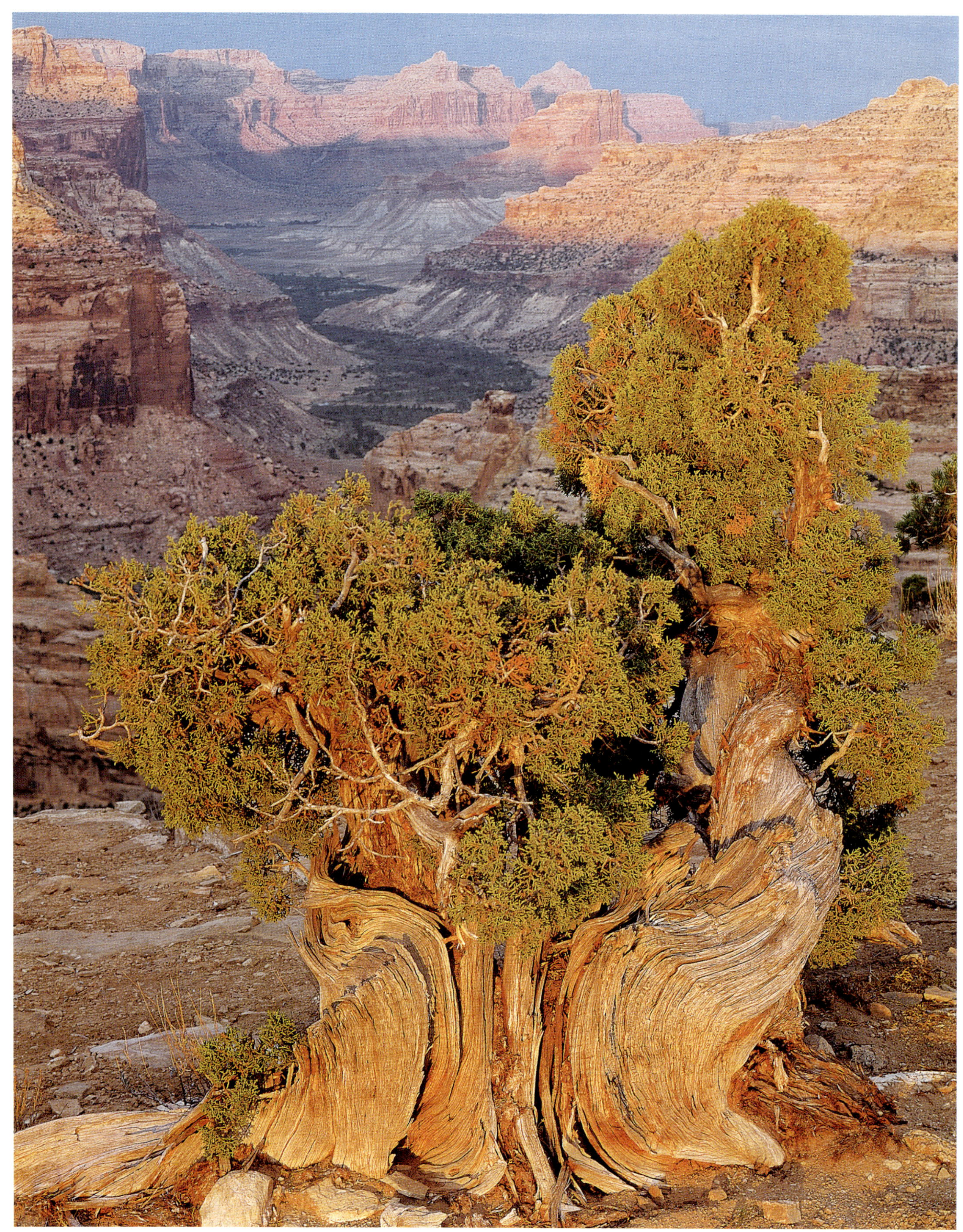

ABOVE: JUNIPER AND SAN RAFAEL RIVER AT THE WEDGE, SAN RAFAEL SWELL. *RIGHT:* NORTH CREEK POOLS, ZION NATIONAL PARK.

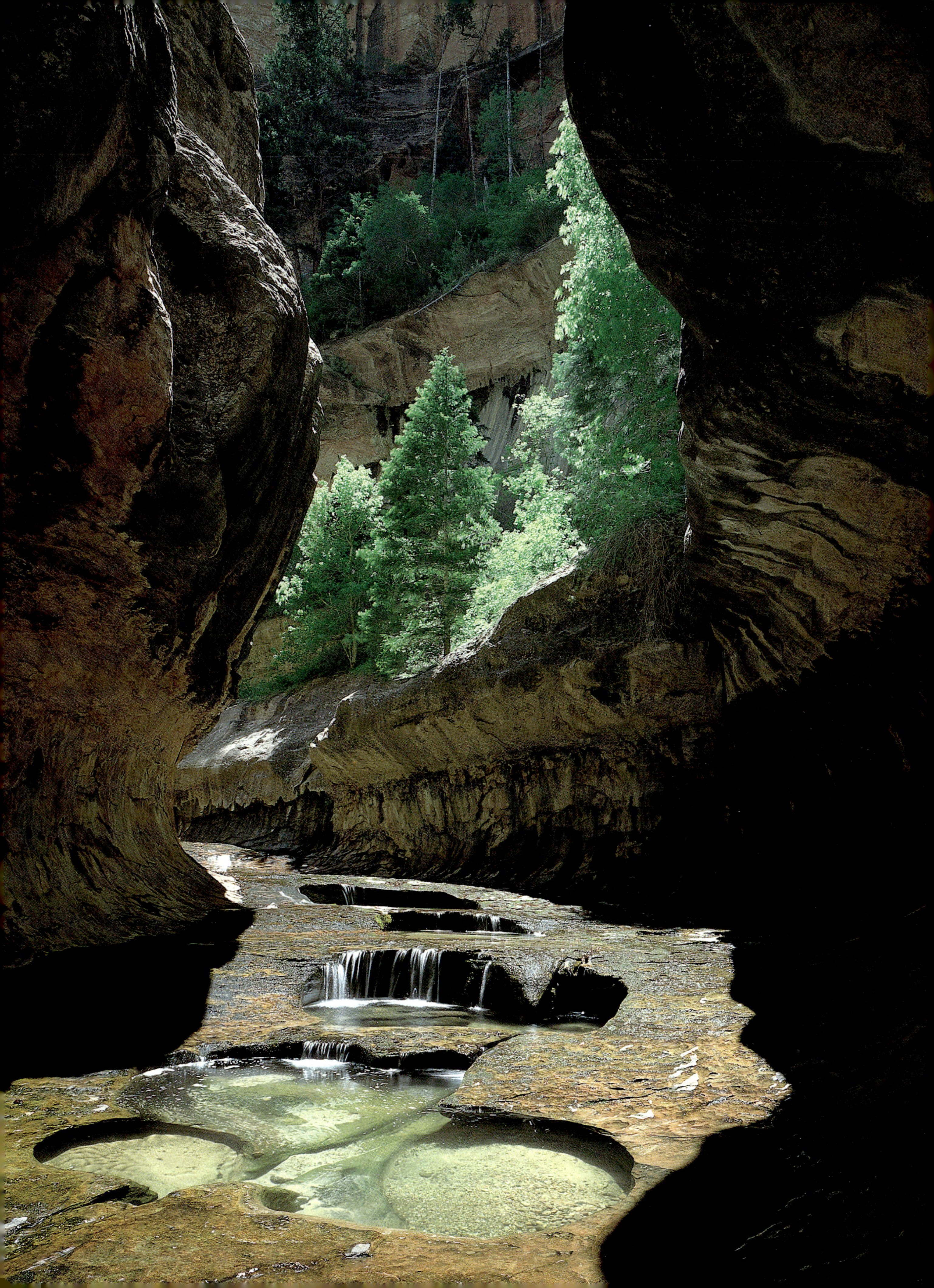

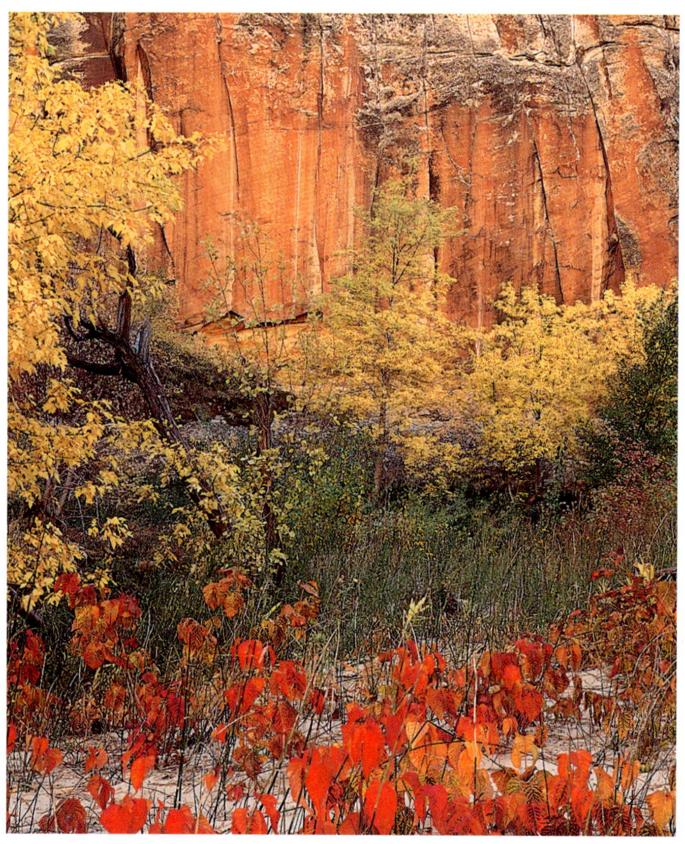

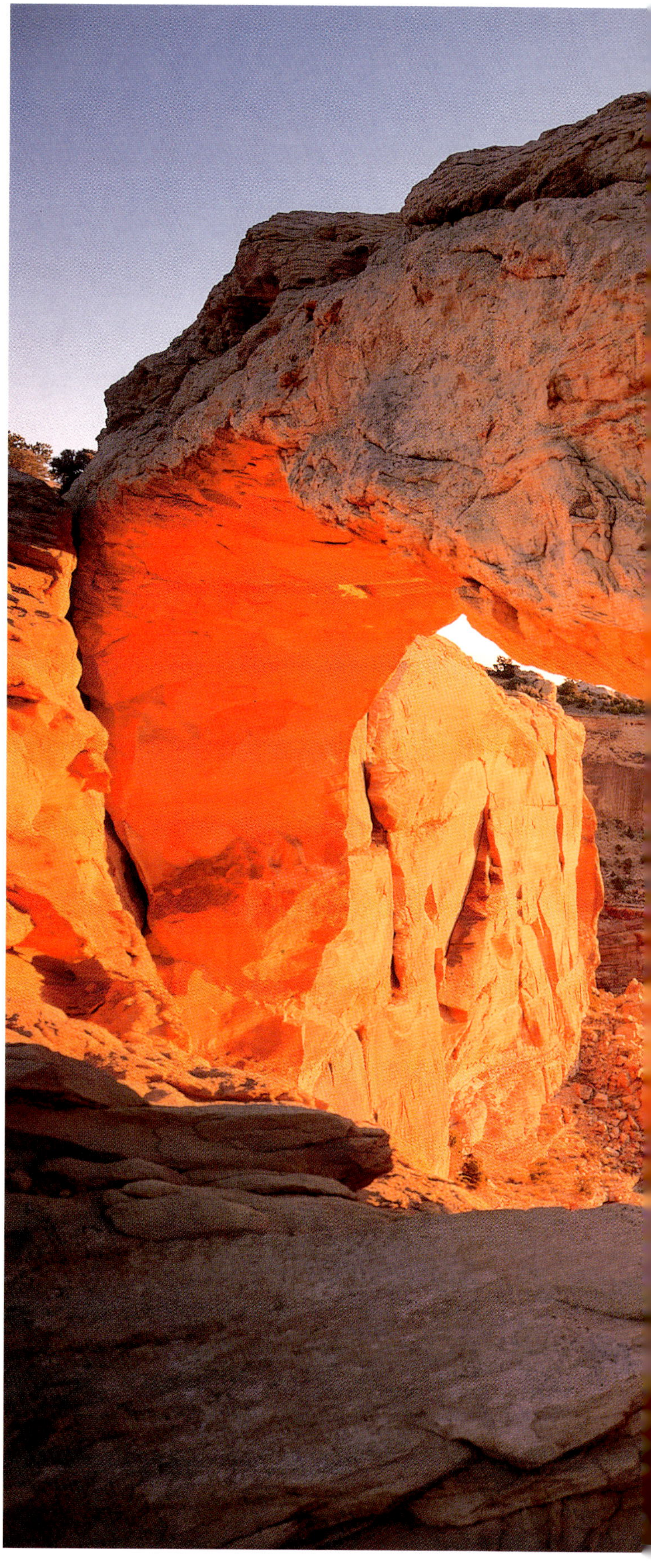

ABOVE: DEATH HOLLOW, ESCALANTE CANYONS,

GRAND STAIRCASE/ESCALANTE NATIONAL MONUMENT.

RIGHT: MESA ARCH AT DAWN, CANYONLANDS NATIONAL PARK.

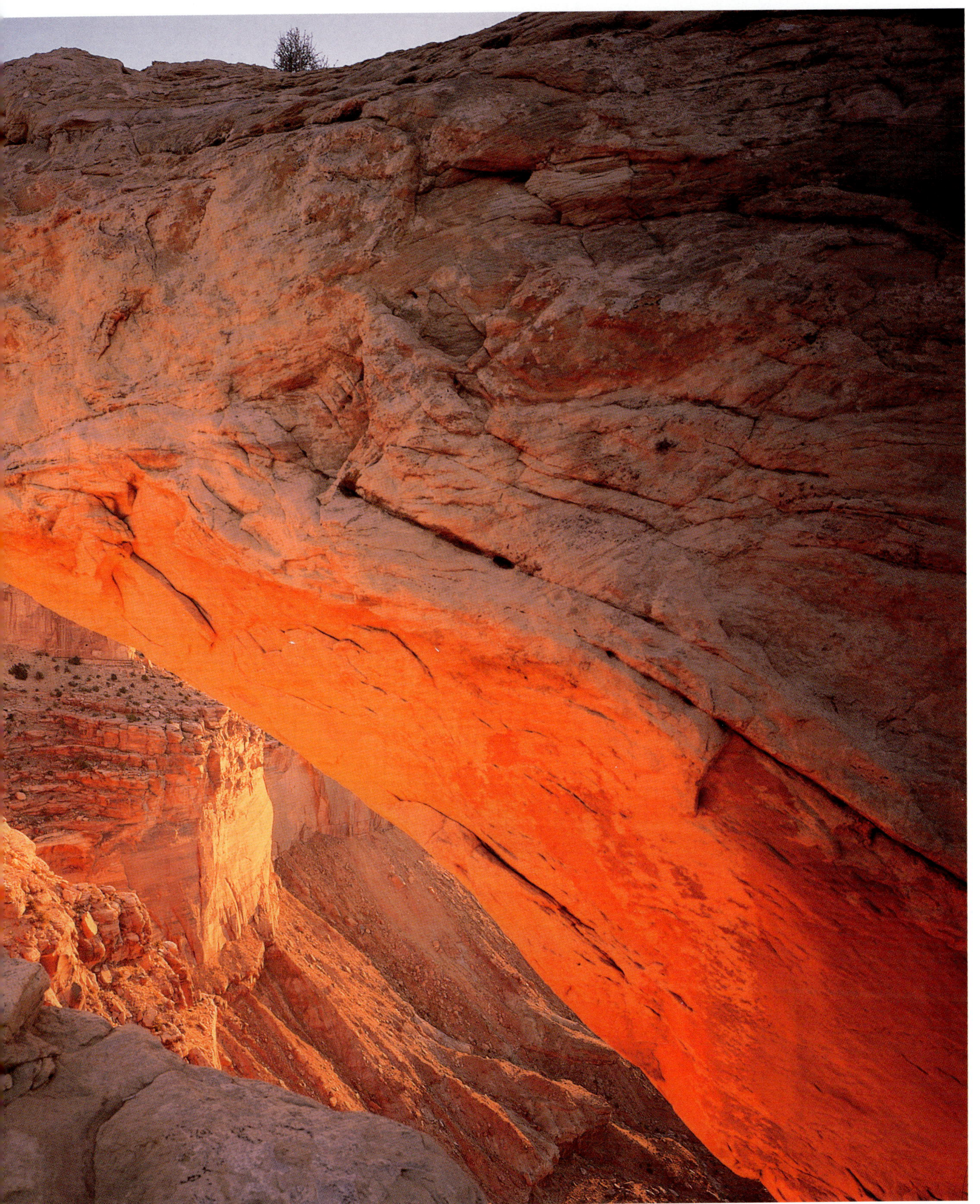

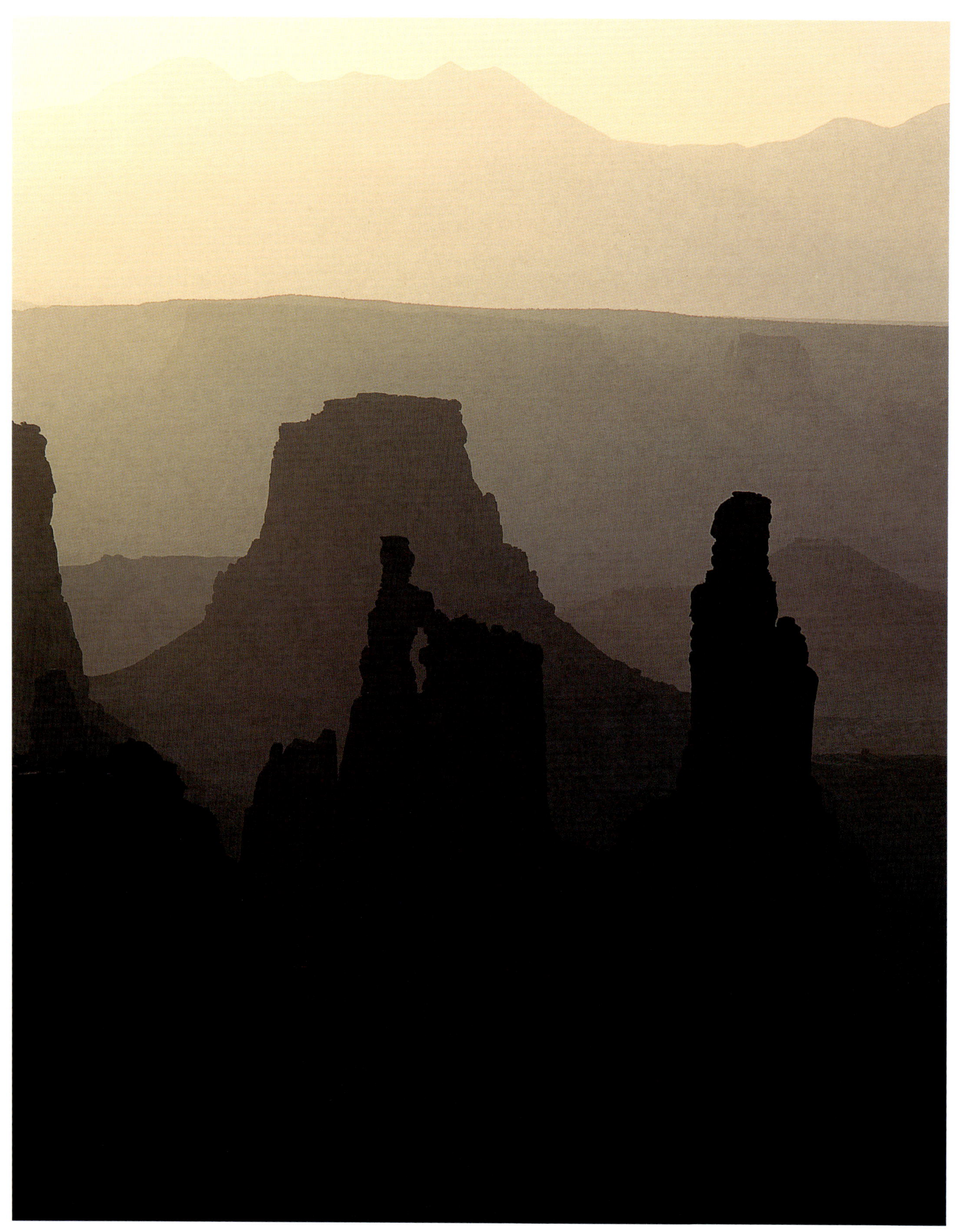

WASHERWOMAN ARCH AND ROCK FORMATIONS BELOW SIERRA LA SAL, IN MORNING LIGHT, CANYONLANDS NATIONAL PARK.

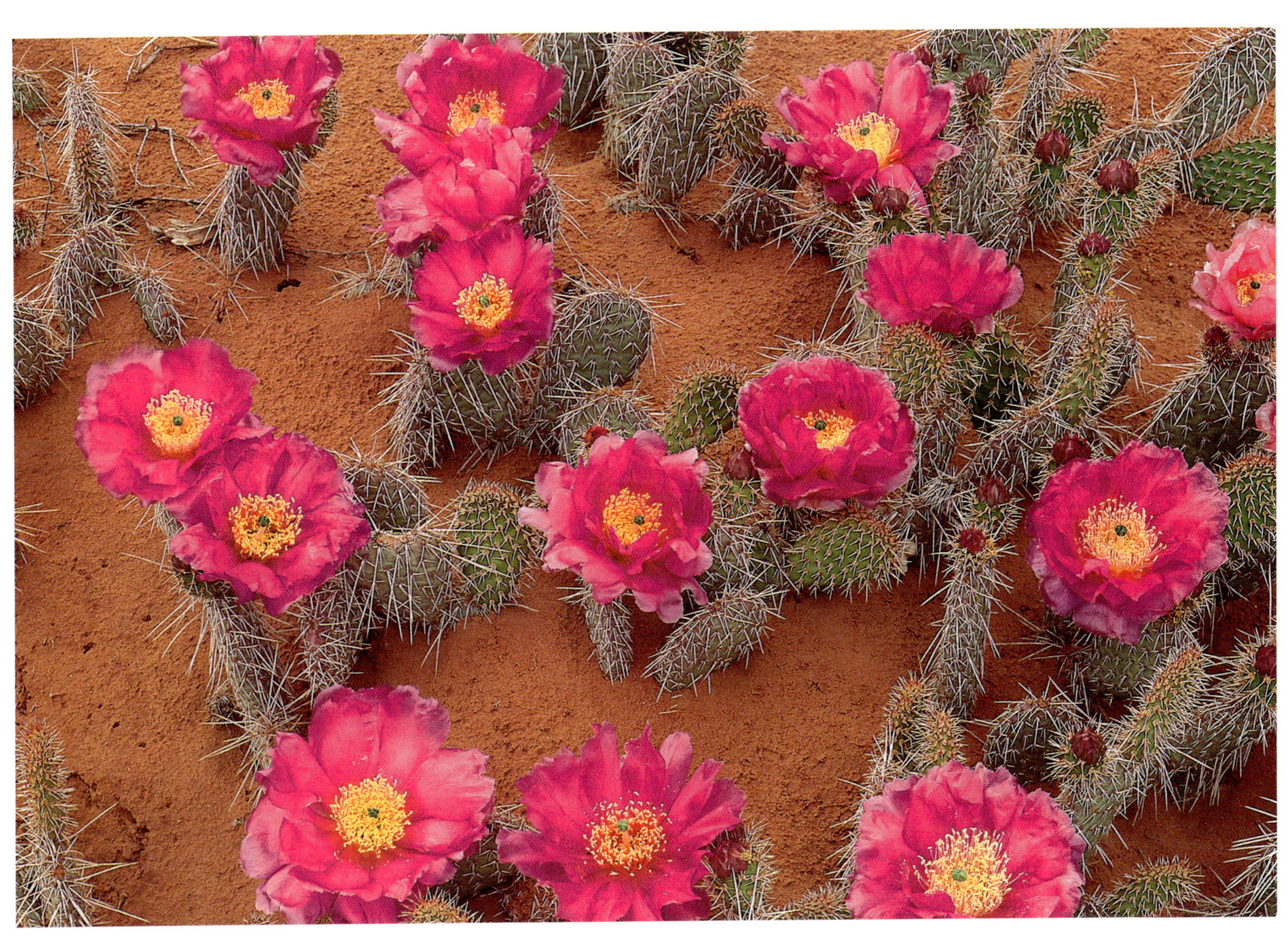

SPRING BLOOMS OF BEAVERTAIL CACTUS ON DESERT SANDS, GRAND STAIRCASE/ESCALANTE CANYONS.

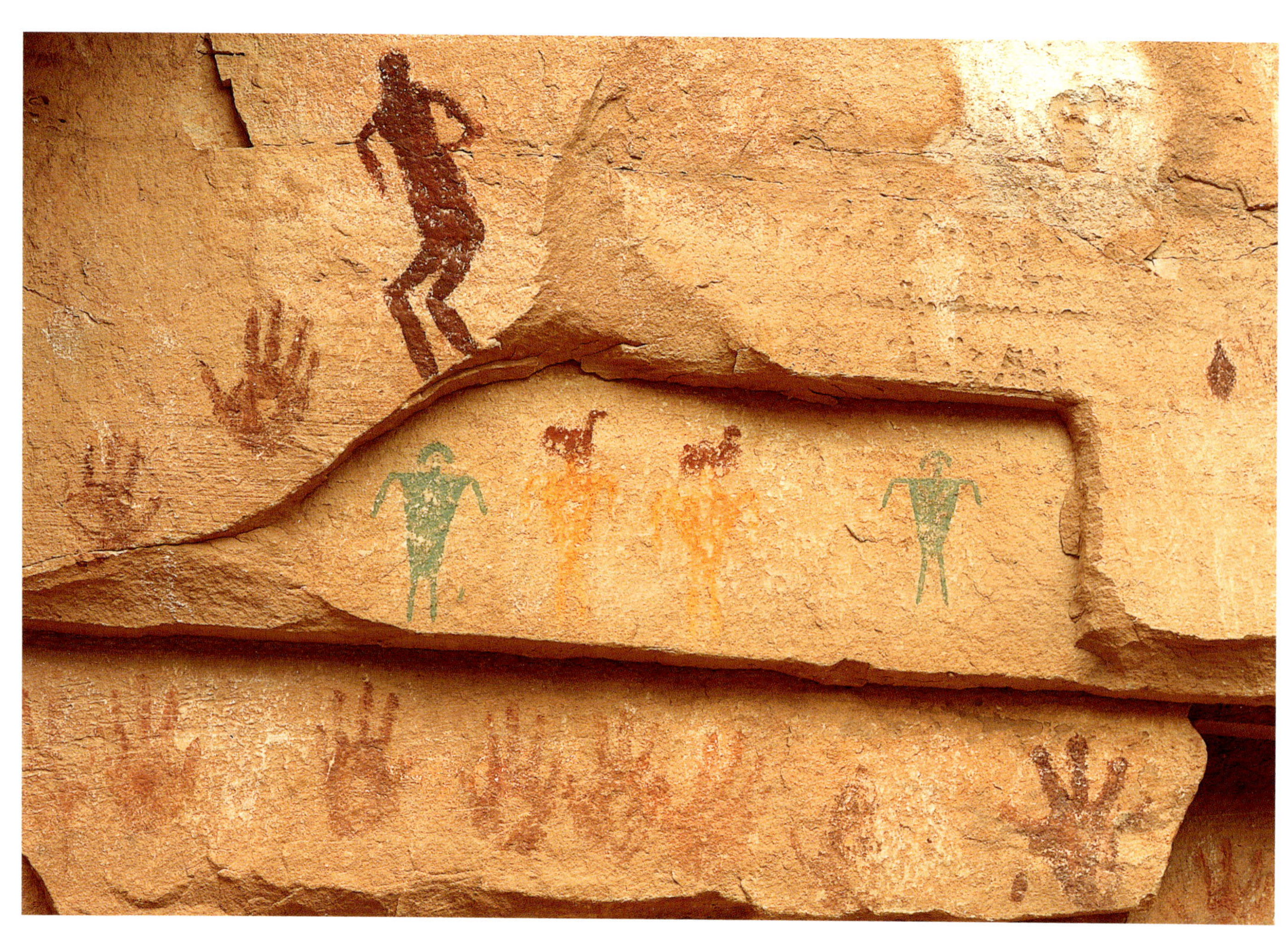

ABOVE: QUAIL PANEL PICTOGRAPH, GRAND GULCH.

RIGHT: COLORADO RIVER, WHITE RIM, CANYONLANDS NATIONAL PARK.

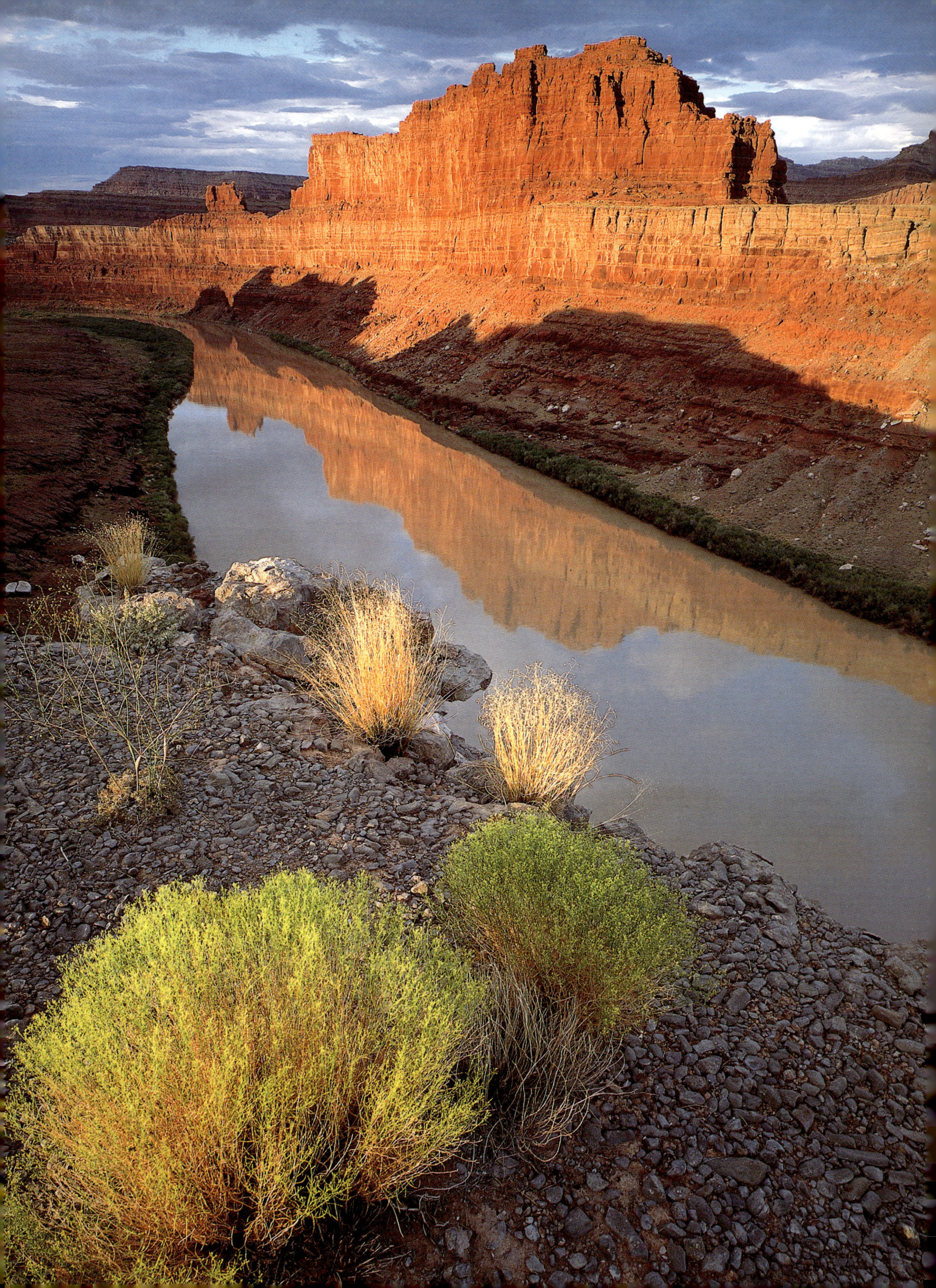

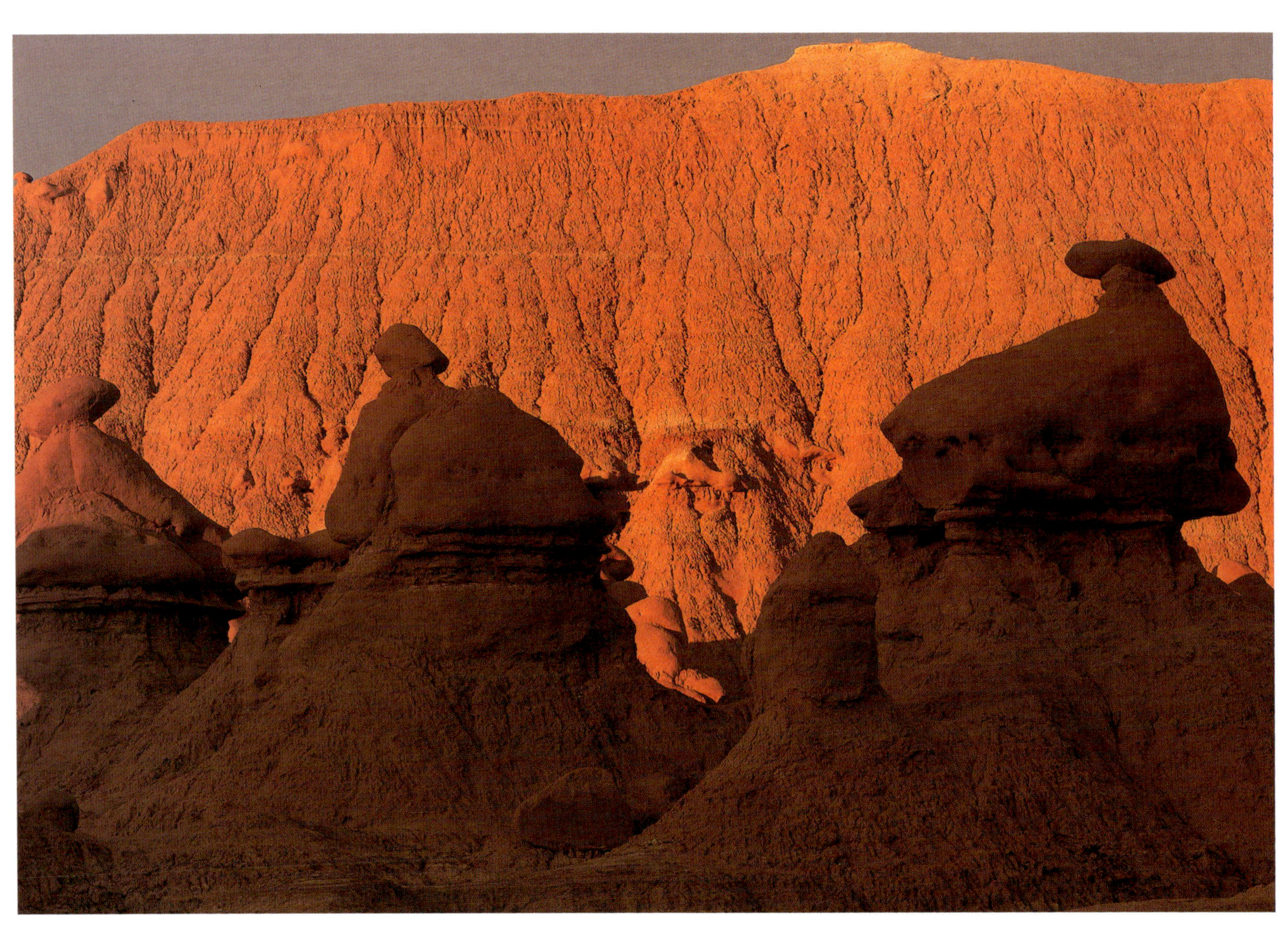

ABOVE: ENTRADA FORMATIONS, GOBLIN VALLEY STATE PARK.

RIGHT: PAINTED HILLS, HENRY MOUNTAINS.

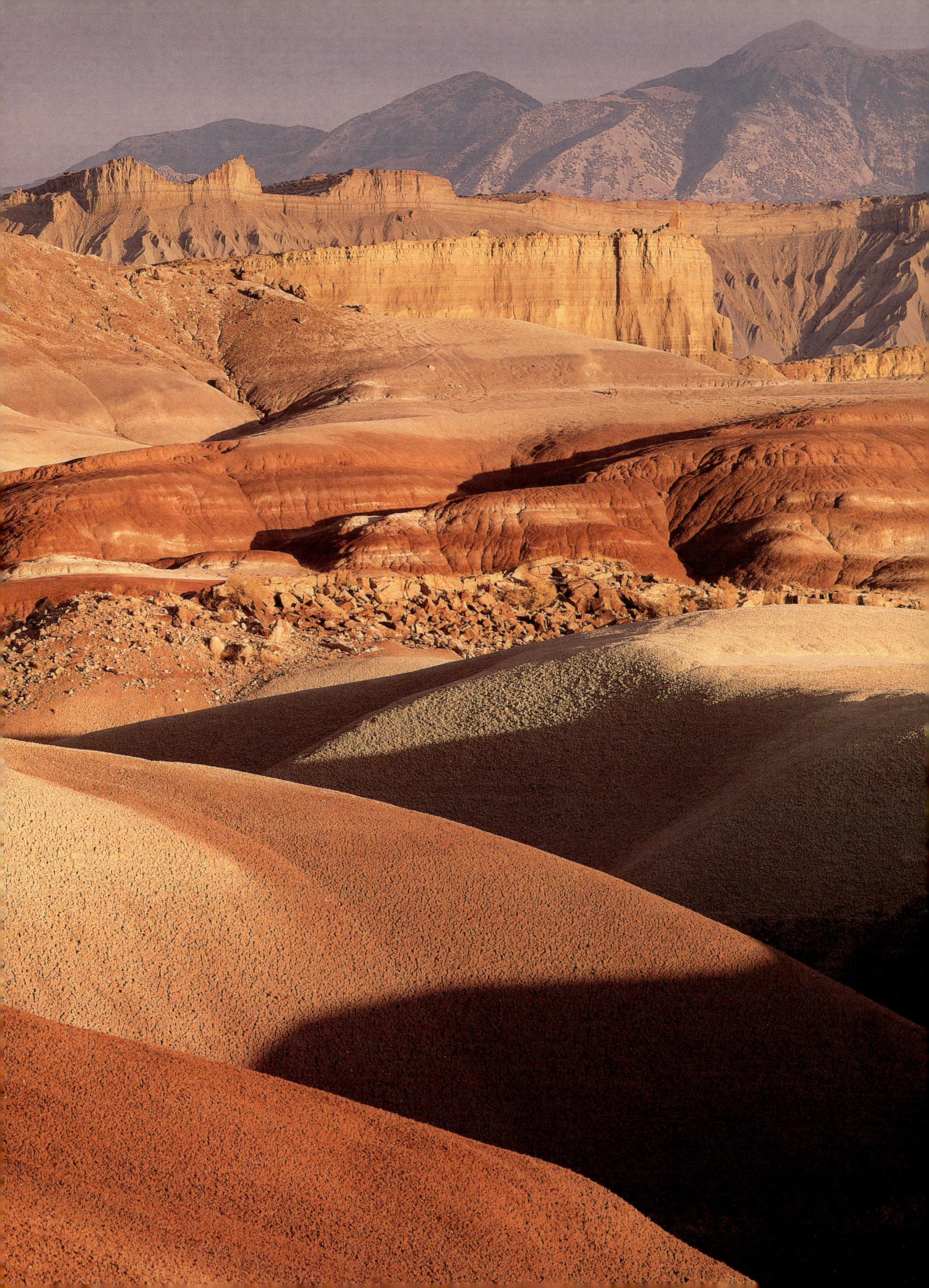

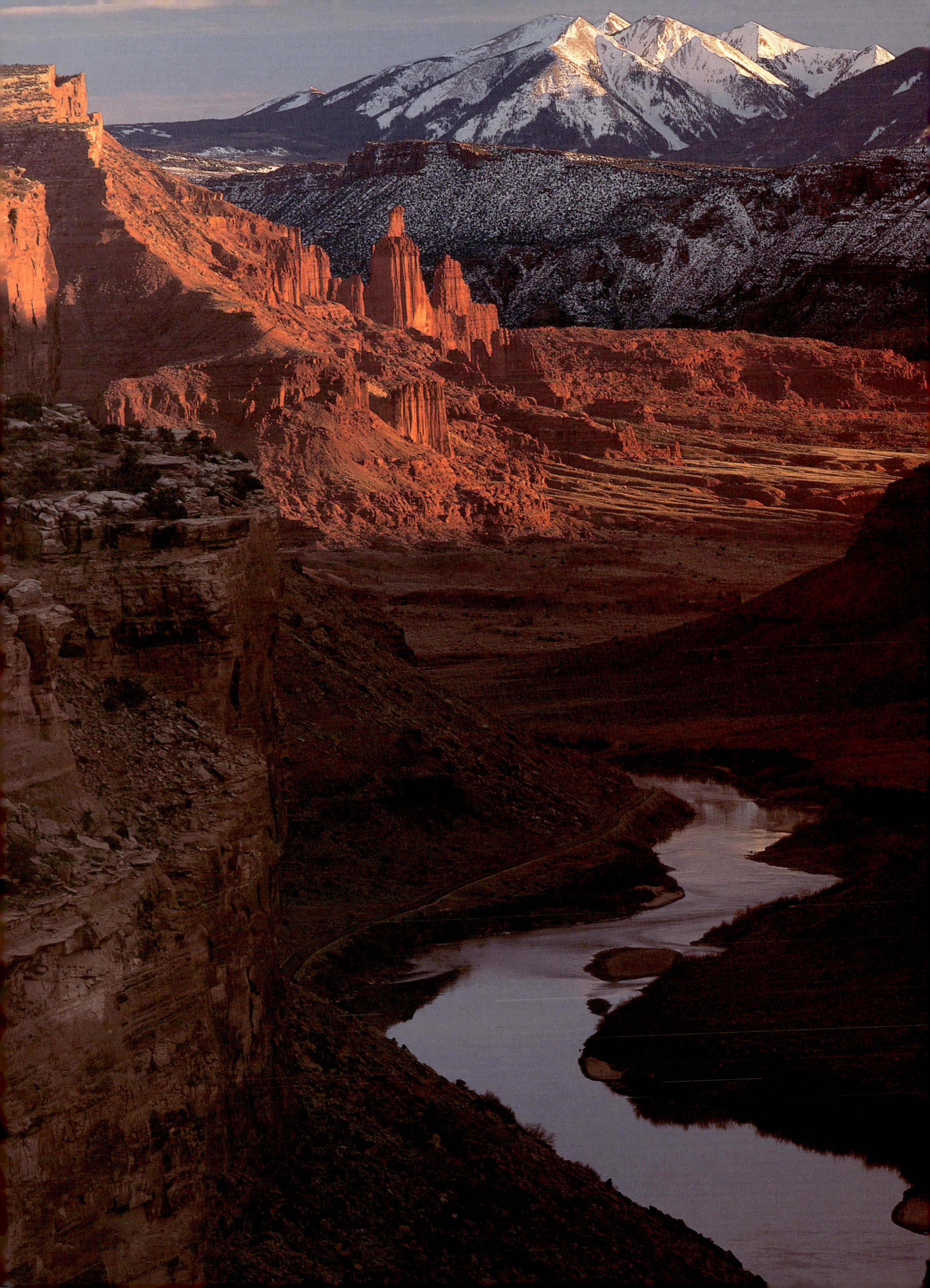

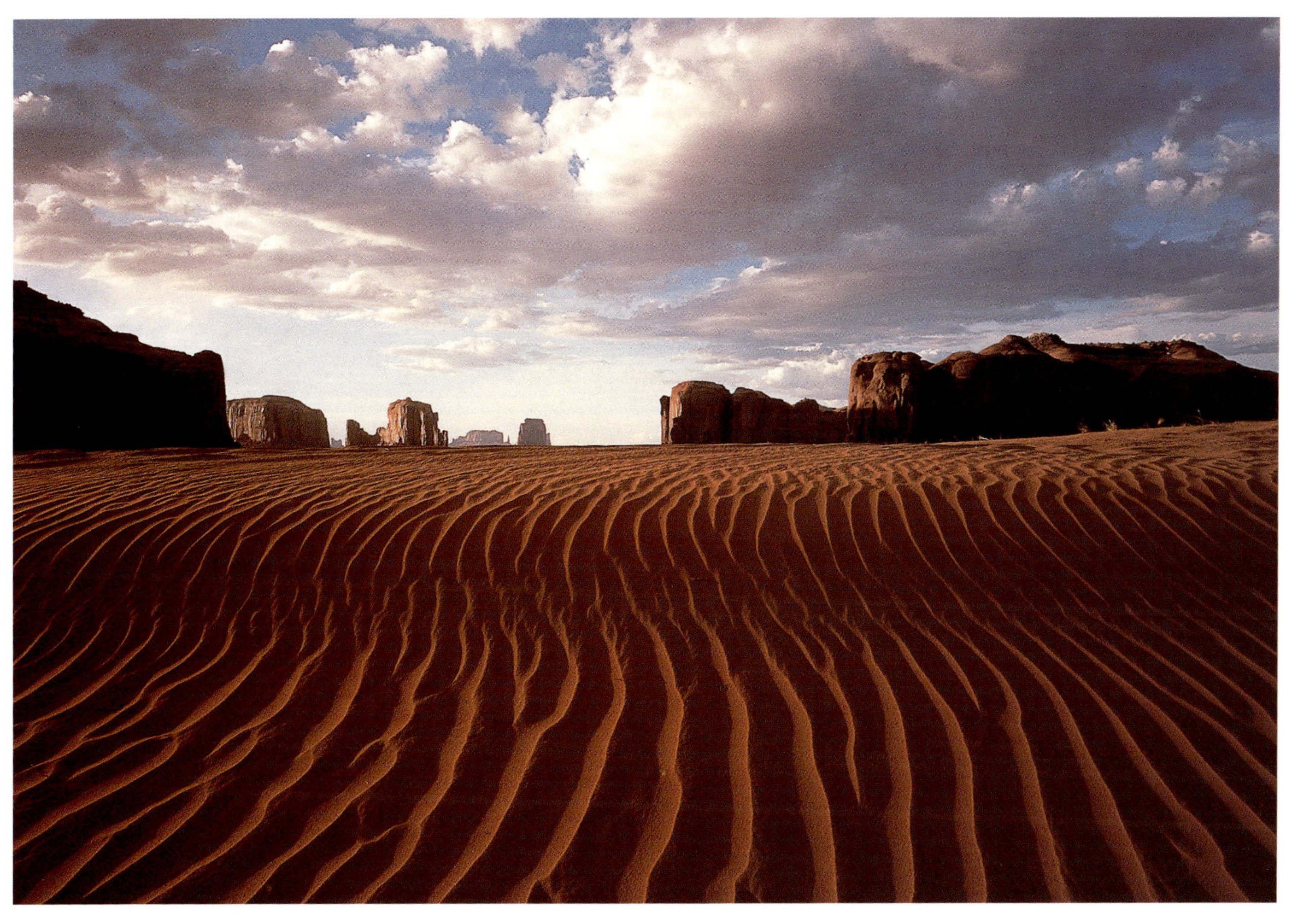

LEFT: FISHER TOWERS AND

SIERRA LA SAL, COLORADO RIVER CANYON.

ABOVE: DUNE RIPPLE CASCADE, MONUMENT VALLEY NAVAJO TRIBAL PARK.

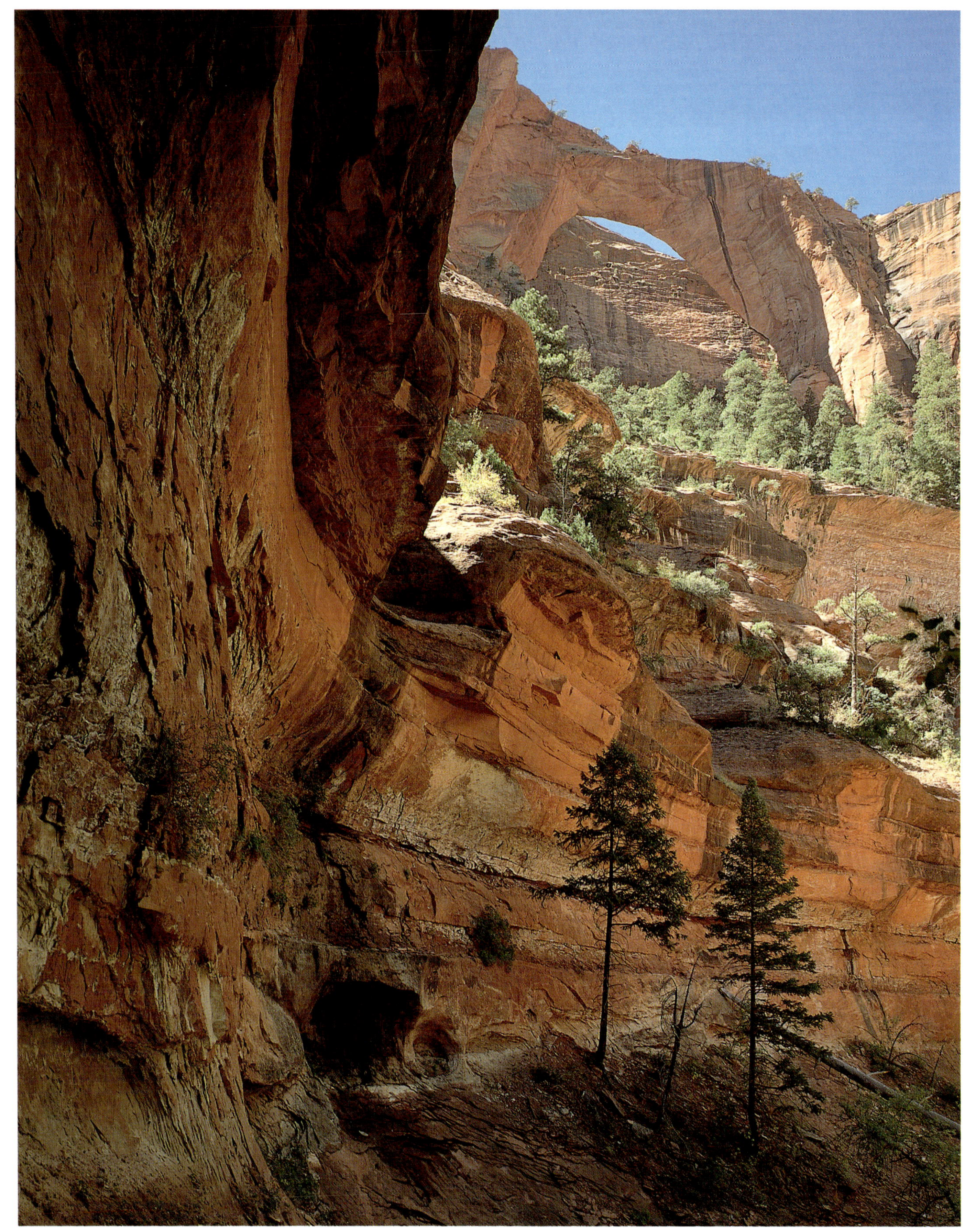

KOLOB ARCH, ZION NATIONAL PARK, WEST.

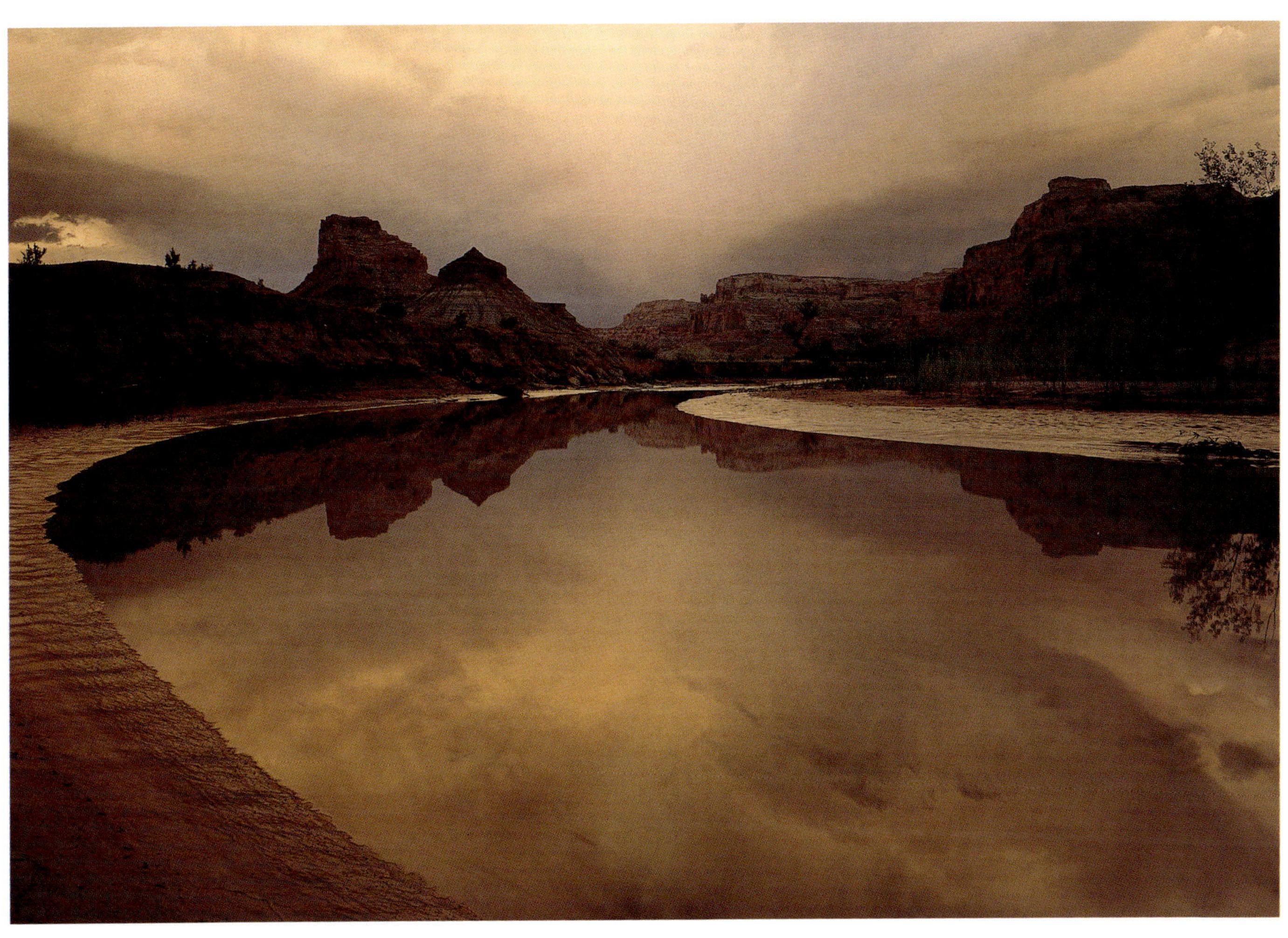

ABOVE: STORM OVER ASSEMBLY HALL AND WINDOW BLIND PEAKS, SAN RAFAEL RIVER, SAN RAFAEL SWELL.

FOLLOWING PAGES: STORMY EVENING EAST OF THE WAH WAH MOUNTAINS,

IN BEAVER COUNTY, BASIN AND RANGE.

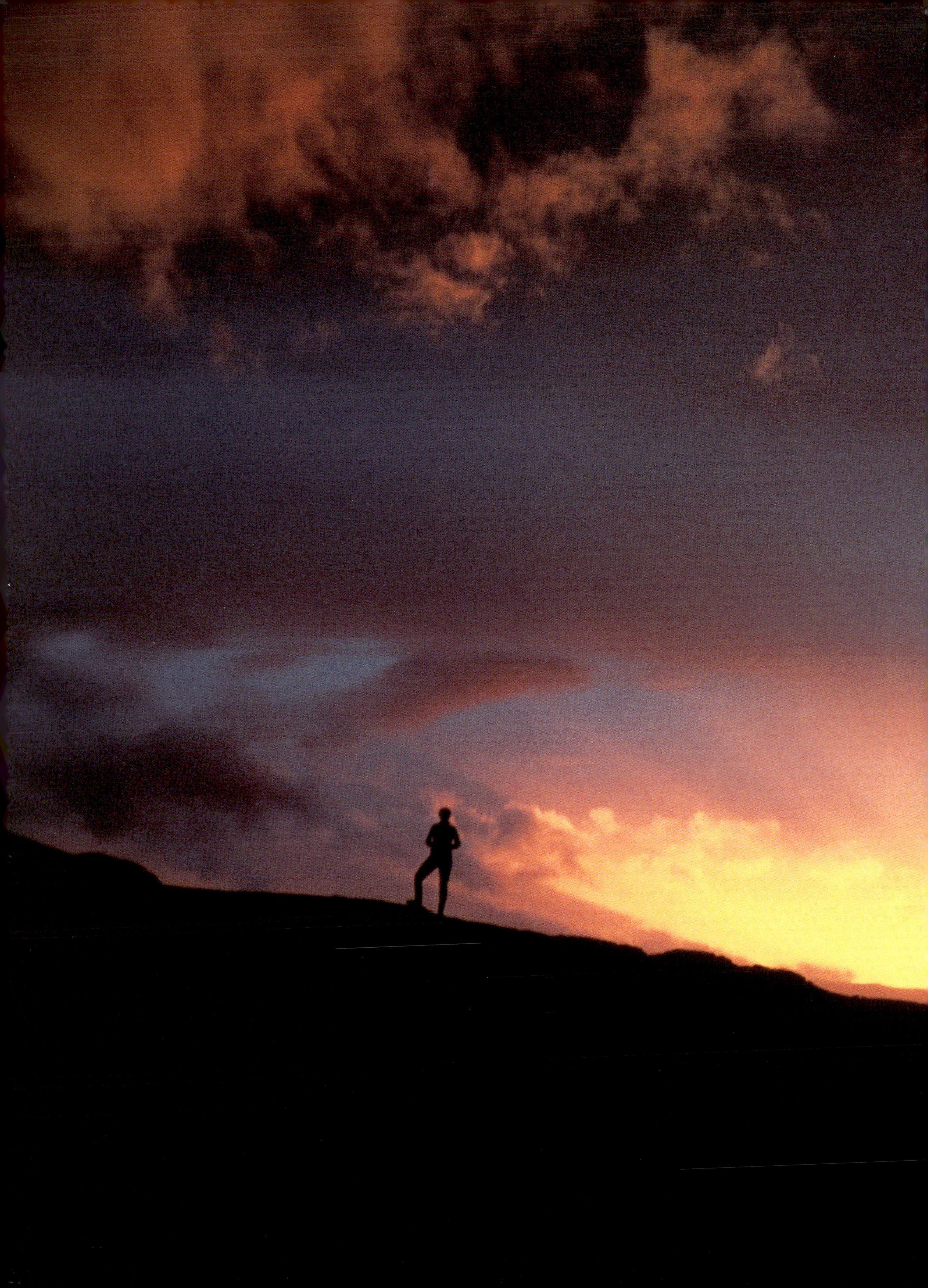

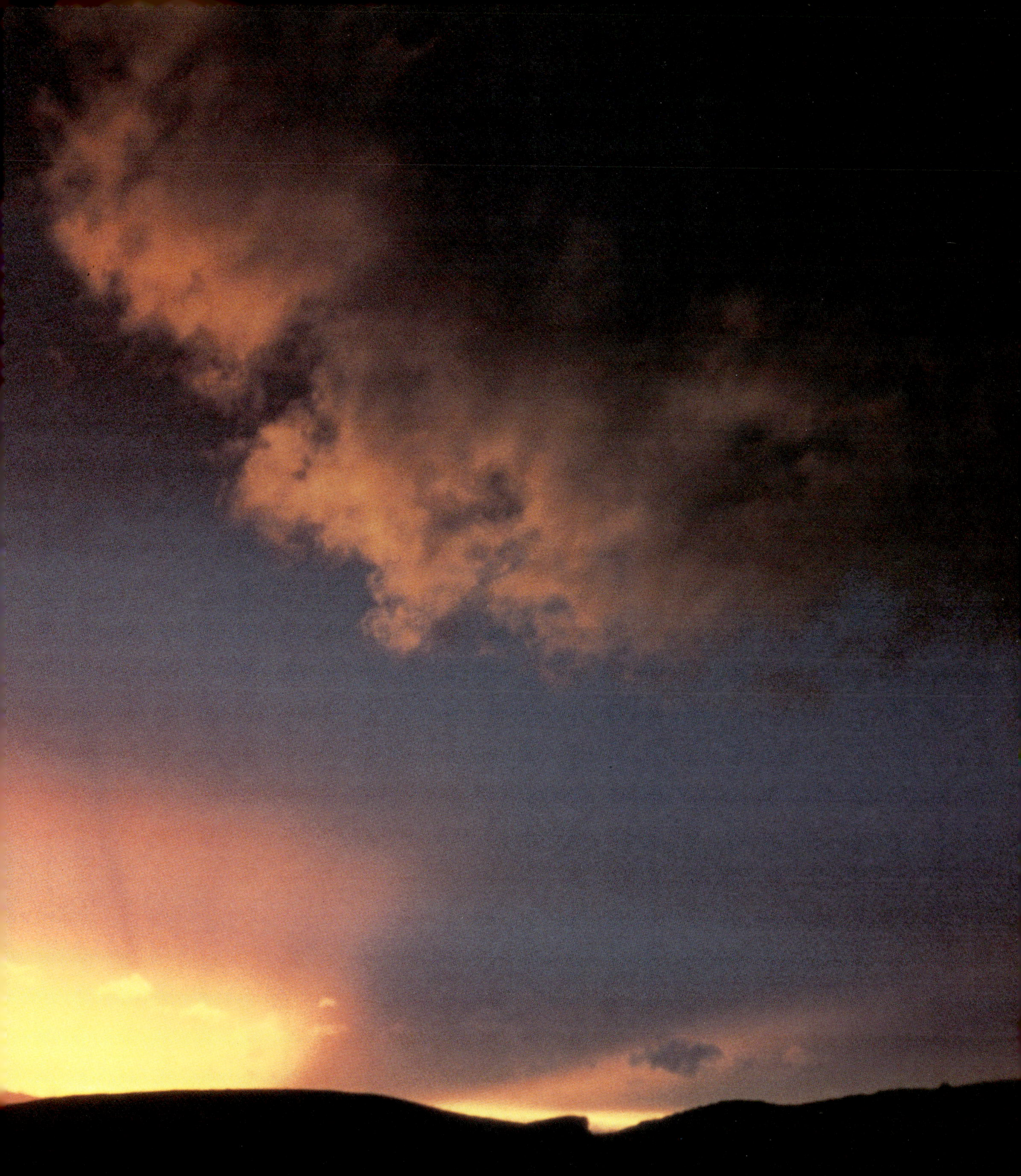

W E S T   D E S E R T

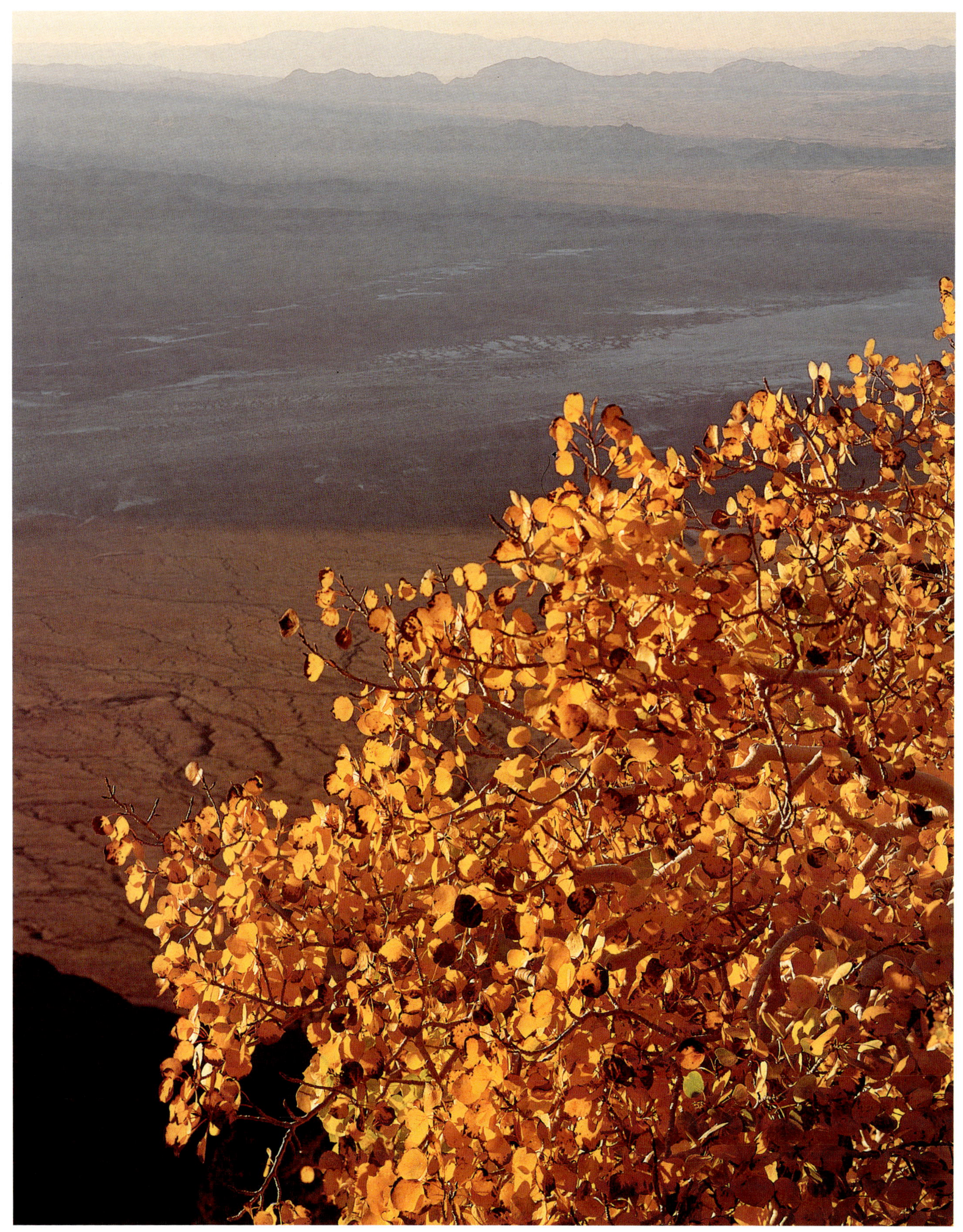

ASPEN, SAN FRANCISCO MOUNTAINS WITH WAH WAH VALLEY.

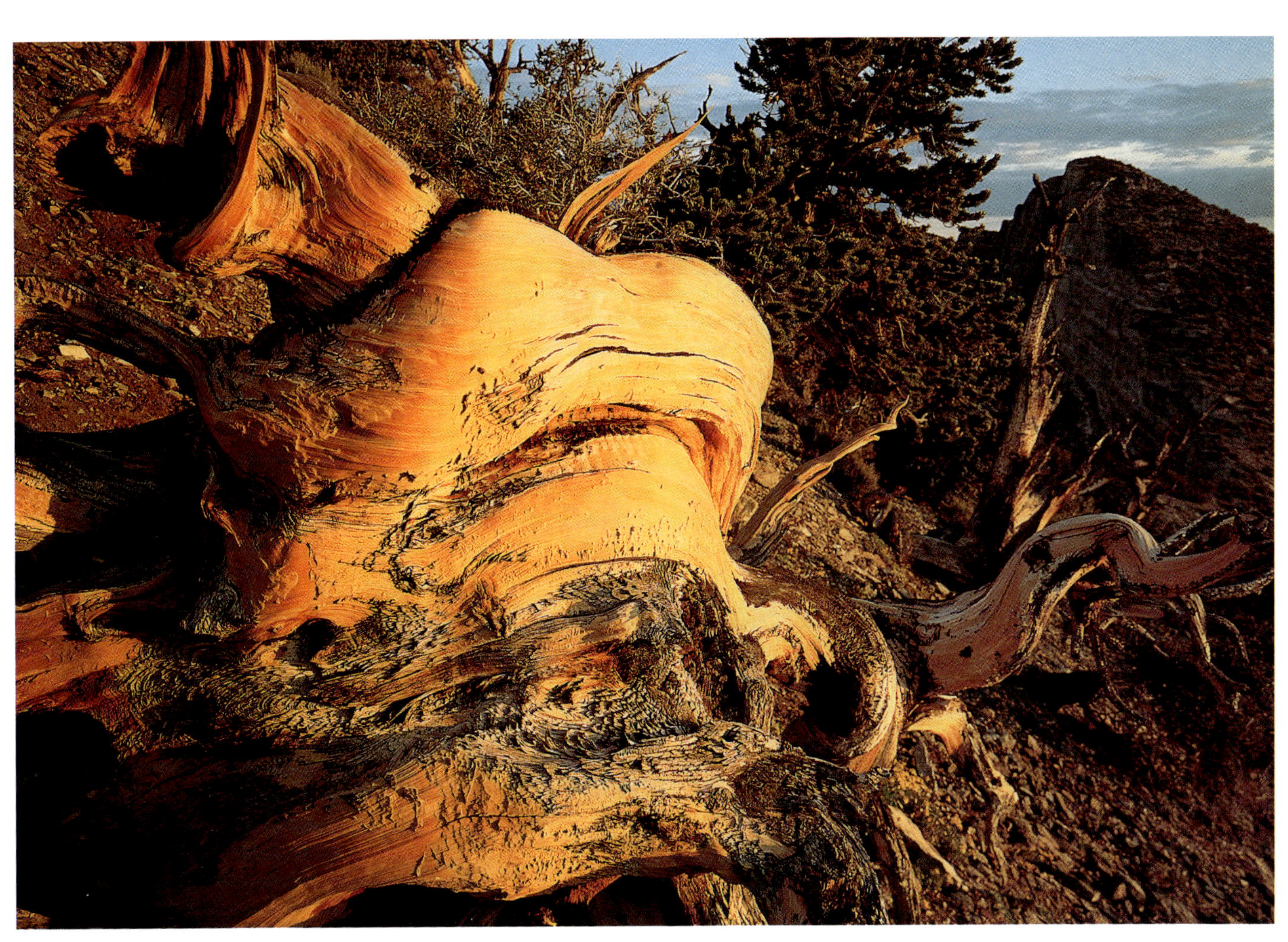

CONTORTED SPRAWL OF ANCIENT BRISTLECONE PINE, HOUSE RANGE.

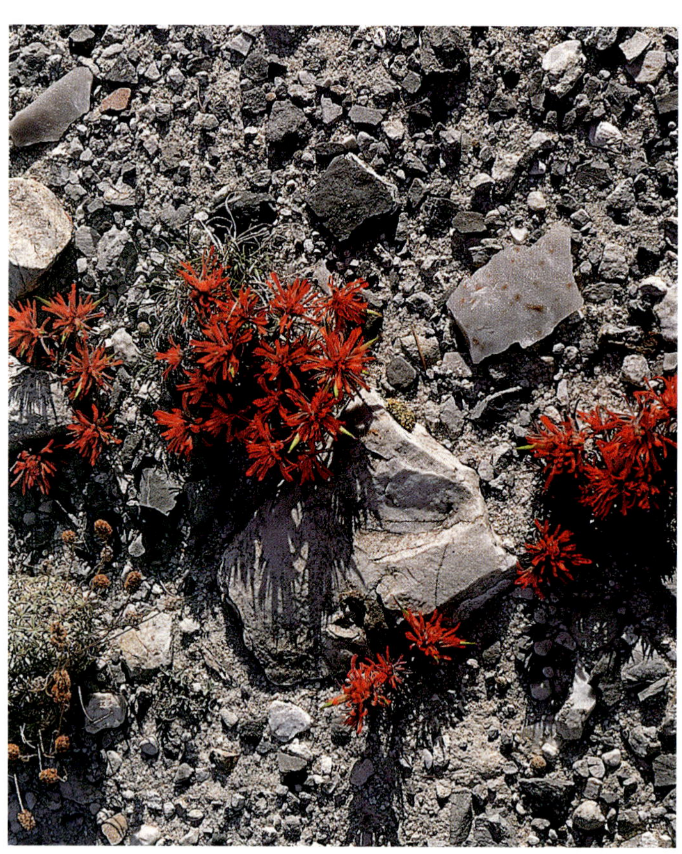

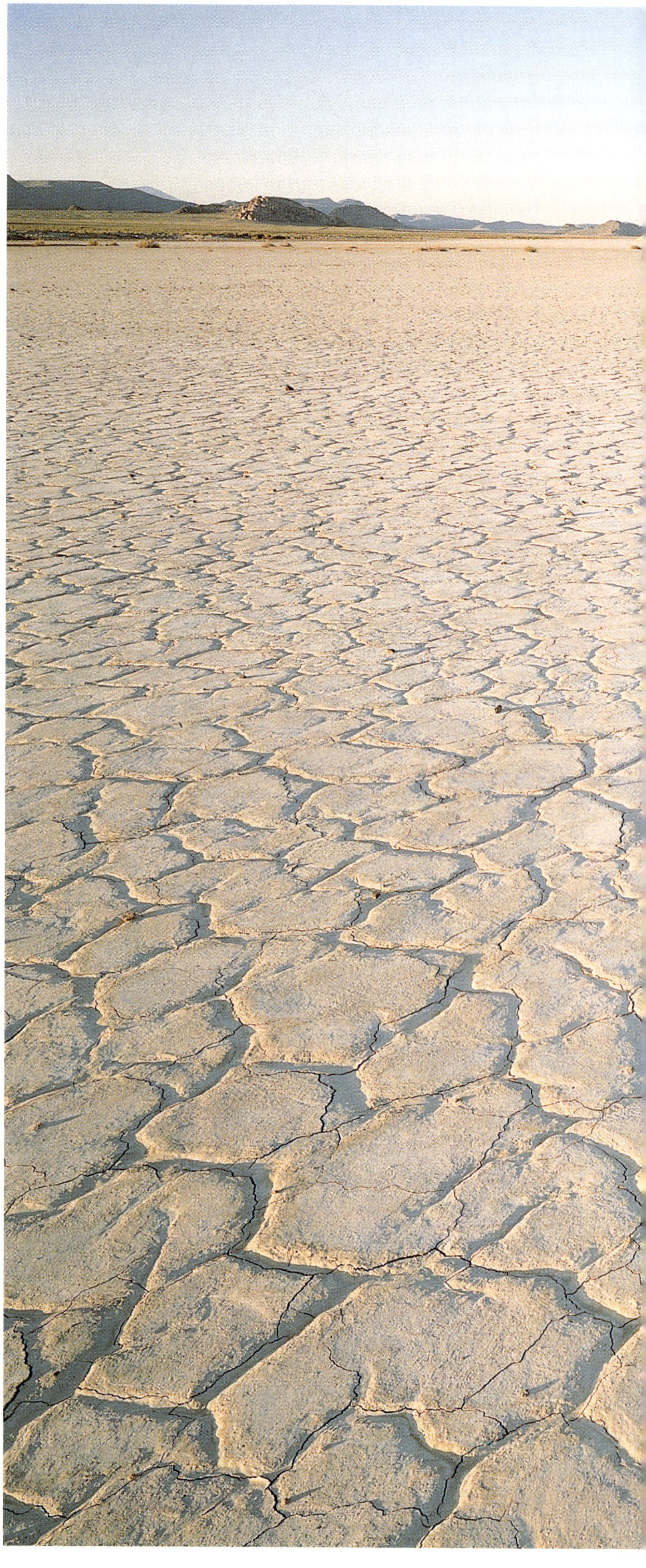

ABOVE: INDIAN PAINTBRUSH AND

ROCKMAT ON SLOPES NEAR CRYSTAL PEAK.

RIGHT: PLAYA IN TULE VALLEY WITH THE CONFUSION RANGE.

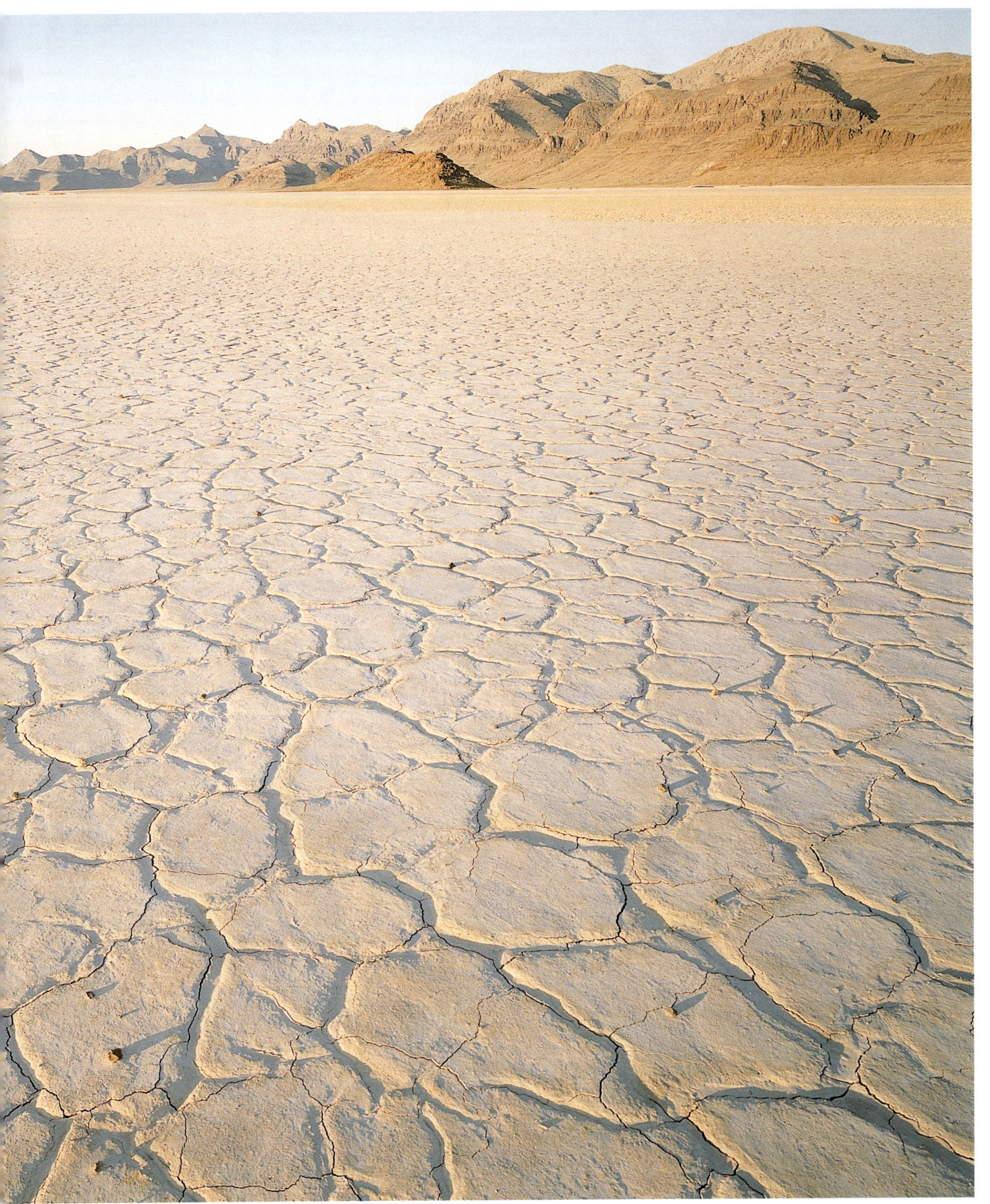

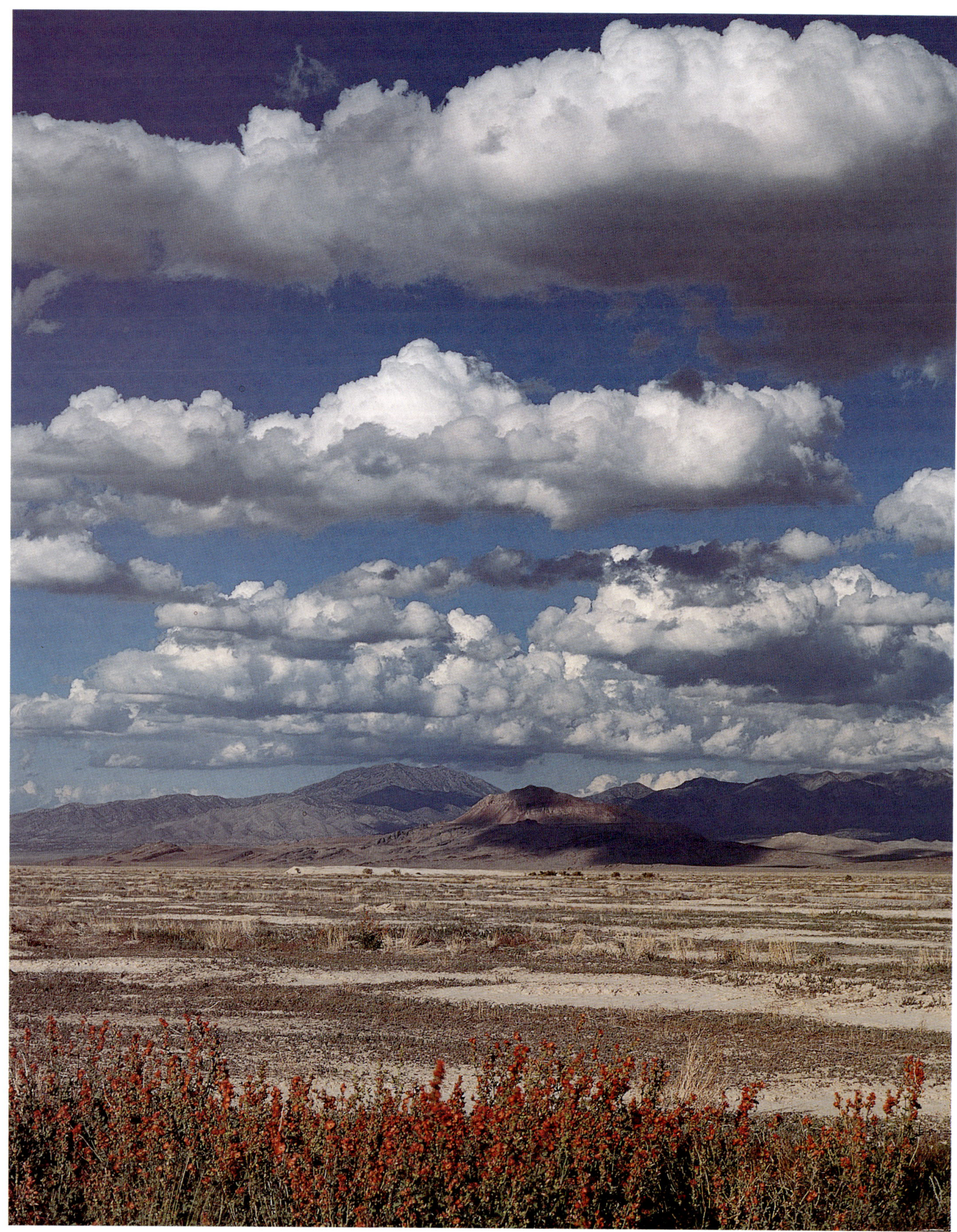

DUGWAY RANGE AND GREAT SALT LAKE DESERT.

Songs beneath the Sands

Coming into Utah from the west, I cross the Nevada-Utah line at Ibapah. Although only 150 air miles southwest of Salt Lake City, it might as well be on the moon. This place on an empty road is distinguished only by being in desolate desert beyond which there is only more desolate desert, without anchor in time or reference in space. Here one enters the southern part of the four-thousand-square-mile Great Salt Desert on the route pioneered by Captain James Hervey Simpson in 1858, later the Pony Express and Stage Route, then the old Lincoln Highway that became Route 40, and finally, this empty, empty road, superceded by new highways farther north and south. Captain Simpson thought it so drear that it looked as if "a gloomy vail or pall had been thrown over it.... No signs of man or beast meet the eye, and even the birds seem to avoid it in their aerial flight."

This salty patch of desert may be one of those places in Utah that is ultimate wilderness, a place so inimical that even the ground squirrel disavows it, even the redtail does not bother to hunt it, and the lizard's throat pulses with heat and no place to hide. No kangaroo rat mound, no kit fox burrow, not even a marauding rattlesnake breaks the bleakness. The only sign of life is a huge, orange-winged Mephistophelian grasshopper that leaps up from the road and pitches crazily into the dusty air.

This terrible emptiness came about when ancient Lake Bonneville (its remnant is the Great Salt Lake) withdrew and left its salts behind as carelessly as a child leaves toys around the room. Alongside the road, the desert undulates with cavernous hollows left by shallow waters that drew up into great waves and scooped out great troughs hundreds of feet long with tens of feet between crests. The troughs can still fill with water in one of the seldom rains. The crests, better drained, permit only scabby plants that can withstand heavy loads of salts, the fat-leafed greasewood, the noxious halogeton, the ubiquitous saltbush—beleaguered, small, scruffy, desperate-looking plants. Most are half dead. They look as if they're sorry they're here and wish it were all over, dropping only enough seed to have a clear conscience about continuing the species.

No matter how hard the surface of the ground is, it still pulverizes into a powdery haze that the wind deposits on everything as if it were positively charged and the object negative. In *Roughing It,* Mark Twain describes how it adhered to everything in his stage coach, flouring eyebrows and moustaches as well as clothes and luggage. On my face, sweat drizzles down through the silt, leaving me looking like a poorly made-up clown, a rag doll fashioned out of dreary muslin, lost in this nightmare of interminable white wilderness where the only animation is a dust devil siphoning up the dust a mile away.

Psychologically the landscape seems all the more bereft because water was once here, a lake as big as Lake Michigan, full of swift, silvery, finny creatures. When the Pleistocene glaciers that bulldozed out the mountains to the north melted, they flooded the low areas. Lake Bonneville expanded and contracted at least ten times, once filling so full it broke through a natural dam and overflowed into the Snake River drainage in Idaho. Geologists extrapolate that the lake dropped fourteen feet that first year, with a flow estimated at one million cfs, a volume inconceivable, a roar unimaginable.

The knowledge that here a surface once shivered and quivered with wind, sparkled and glinted with sunlight, gives this light-absorbent landscape a particular dusty deathliness, like moth wings in the throat.

Stringing back westward on the old Pony Express route, my attention has been riveted on the Fish Springs Range ahead, peaks haloed with afternoon light, valleys illuminated with a gentle glow, the softening blues and greens creating a peacefulness for the eye in contrast to the flats that seem to go on a hard, monotonous forever. The mountains beckon respite from everything that plagues these silent, bleak lands.

As the day shutters down, oxymoronic glints of water and verdant dashes of color in this ultimate desert don't make sense; neither does the gabbling and whooping, calling and shrilling, quacking and warbling, a constant rustle of sound that entwines into individual calls and then coalesces again into a cacophony of bird essays on the necessity of water: Fish Springs.

The series of ponds at this national wildlife refuge has such a variety of birds that it's like thumbing through an illustrated field guide. A black-crowned night heron with red eyes stands on the bank of the first pond. Barn swallows hurtle into the sky. Savannah sparrows busy themselves in the brush. A pair of Canadian geese waddles along the ground with their goslings strung between them. Two ruddy ducks bob at each other. The extravagance of birds in such an assertive desert is astounding: snowy egrets and willets, greater yellowlegs, killdeer and pied-billed grebes, avocets and yellow-headed blackbirds. The mix of ducks alone is remarkable: cinnamon and green-winged teal, mallards and canvasbacks, pintails and gadwalls. Two Wilson's phalaropes paddle circles in the water, the male drab, the female brightly colored. The comely redlegged stilts walk in water up to their "knees," lifting each leg in an elegantly exaggerated manner, a movement dainty but imperious.

At suppertime, the sun gathers behind a peak. Light shafts through breaks in the phalanx of mountains, paints four Naples yellow stripes down the valley, outlines the clouds in platinum. As the sun lowers, the clouds phase to peach, then become fire opals, jeweling the sky, pulsing streamers of light. To the south, two lenticular clouds like two trumpet fish in a silvery sky—blue gray backs, rosy bellies—swim south, one ahead of the other. They disintegrate into fossils, disappear in layers of time.

The sun settles below the rim. Light sinks into the mountain valleys, to be held there until tomorrow, an earth bringing forth itself every morning, gathering itself in every evening. Short rhythms of day and night, larger rhythms of season, millennial rhythms that the human span cannot encompass blend, while the fading light makes sense of infinity.

In the autumn, I enter northeastern Utah from Wyoming, take the first turnoff that looks interesting and end up on the summit of a high hill called Mount McKinnon. The summit commands a view of valleys and ridges to the east, reiterated, as if whoever designed this view, discontent with the finished product, kept proliferating ridges, compulsively adding just one more. Distance levels and subdues them in color, and I look out over places named Sugar Pine Canyon and Zeke Hollow and Peggy Hollow Spring. To the southeast, through a breach in the hills, a ruffle of Uinta Mountain peaks shows, the only major mountain range in the United States to run east and west, although its stark, silvery, crystalline granites and huge domings of molten igneous rock were pushed up at the same time as the predominantly north-south Rocky Mountains.

I zip my jacket against the chill of early October and hug myself to keep from shivering. In my mind's eye, I see a favorite summer meadow high in the eastern Uintas, a flow of green that reached from horizon to horizon. There were multitudes of flowers and a sense of summer so strong I invoke its heat, and the memory comes to warm me on this gelid day years later.

On top of the mountain, at this altitude and latitude, cold winds prune and stunt the big sagebrush, leaving tufts of gray green on bare, scraggly black branches. The seedheads' tall brown spikes tick like metronomes in the crisp breeze, and the stiff big sagebrush branches scarcely move. The grasses beneath twitch. A fly, immobilized with wind and cold, nestles in a late dandelion and does not move even when I lean close to look at it, nose to antennae.

Big puffy clouds blossoming from the west mark a front coming in. The buffeting wind confirms it. As clouds clot the sky, they isolate the sunlight into a series of spotlights snapping on and off across the ridges, burnishing a rim of dull yellow aspen to brilliant gold, then sweeping on to the next ridge, as if the sun were moving, not the clouds. An aspen clone, with leaves colored a deep vermilion orange, still holds its leaves, surrounded by empty-leaved trees that feather the slope like pewter wings. When wind and light catch the leaves, the leaves glisten, and their fluttering animates the morning with arpeggios of light.

The scrub oak on Mount McKinnon is in all stages of fall color. A few still hold summer's green, but most progress from tan to copper to mahogany, culminating in resonant patches of alizarin, ranging from stunted shrubs to scabby-trunked, short-twigged trees that scratch at the wind. A leafless scrub oak pushes a dozen stems out of one base, branches crisscrossing in short arcs, branches with a proliferation of twigs that fill its airspace with curves and quirks. A black fungus thickens many branches so that they look fire-scarred, pulls off the bark, and exposes the inner wood. The last browned leaves cling and curl like little hands gesticulating, describing the season, talking about winter.

Sand Creek is a little drizzle of a stream in eastern Utah that leaks into the Green River below Ouray. Not quite two hundred miles above the confluence of the Green and Colorado Rivers, it marks the northern entrance to Desolation and Gray Canyons where I will begin a trip as a consultant of the Museum of Northern Arizona.

I think of this reach of the Green as the river's middle child. Upstream are the high cirques where the river begins, the glaciers through which water at the freezing point corkscrews, the high meadows and flat valleys through which it meanders, and magnificent, rapid-filled canyons etched into the Uinta Mountains. Downstream there are no more rapids, the galloping excitement of whitewater replaced by the stillness and peacefulness of Labyrinth and Stillwater Canyons. Desolation and Gray, still tatted with frothing rapids, are also graced with a visual serenity of walls and cliffs. Desolation and Gray are remote (there are no settlements on the river between the towns of Ouray and Green River), a little aloof, working out

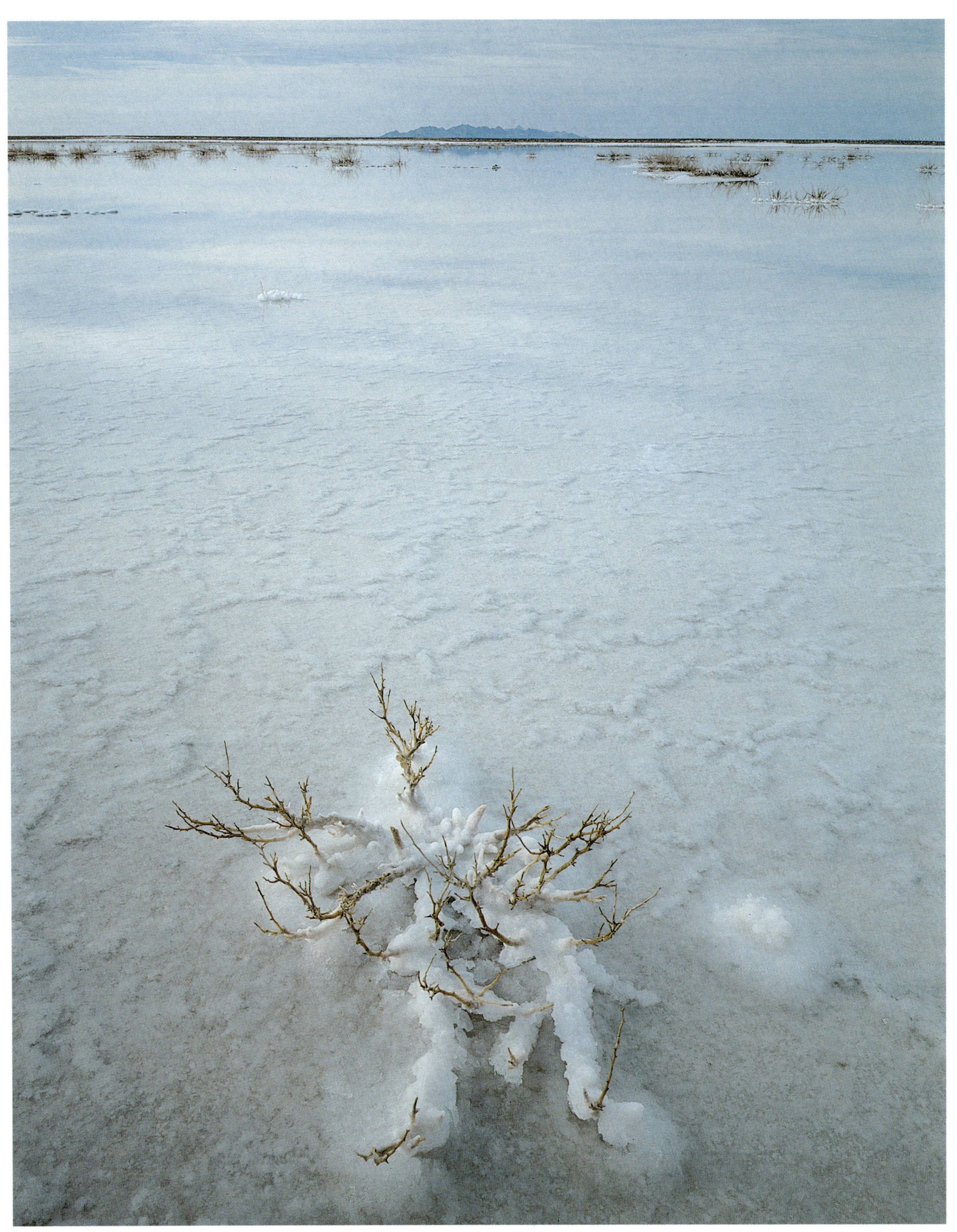

SALT-ENCRUSTED PLANT, FLOATING ISLAND, GREAT SALT LAKE DESERT.

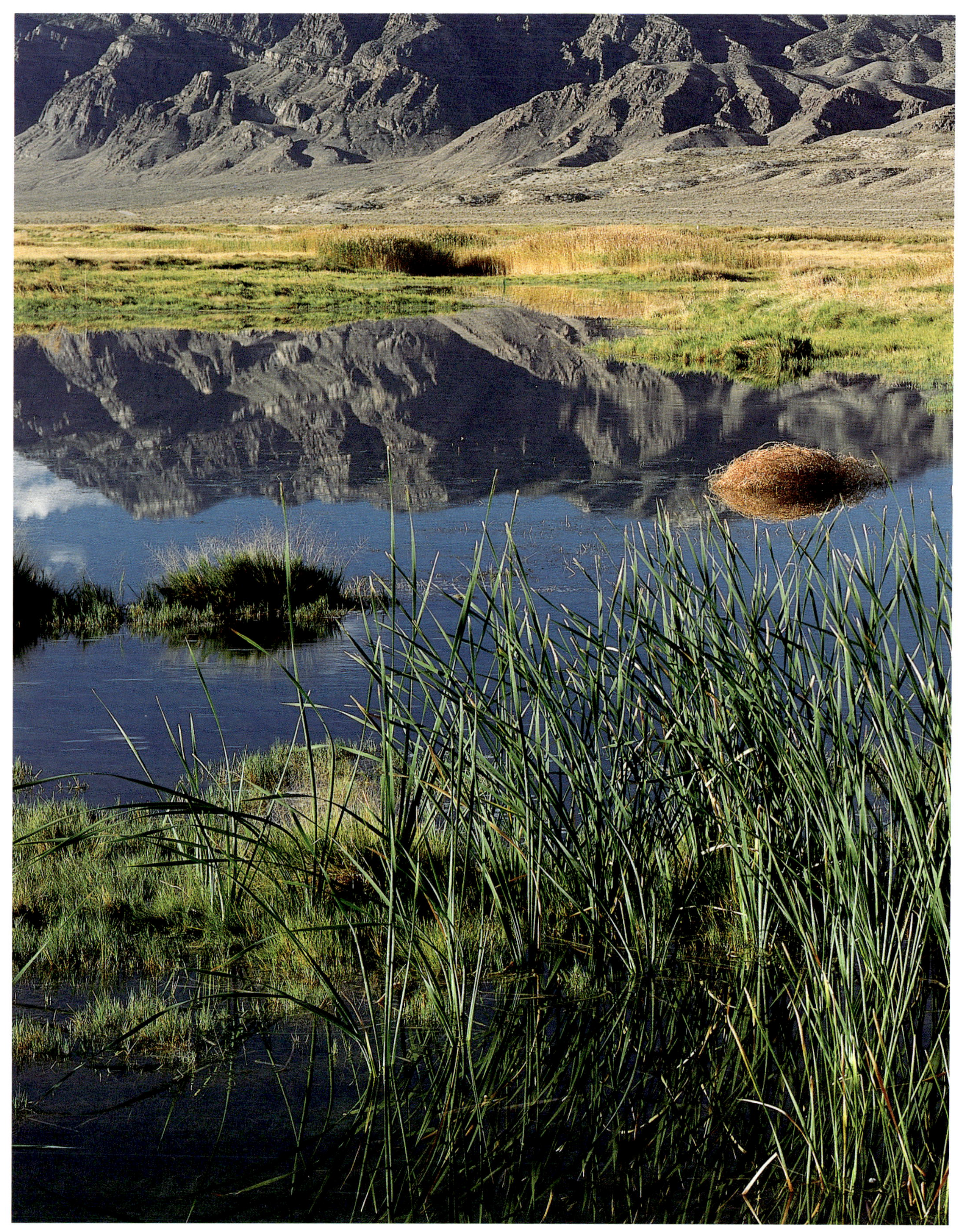

FISH SPRINGS NATIONAL WILDLIFE REFUGE, GREAT SALT LAKE DESERT.

their secrets in their own way, with their own special, subtle, and astounding beauty.

Most outfitters airlift passengers from Green River to Sand Creek to avoid a long, roundabout drive. At the Green River Airport, the orange wind sock hangs mercifully limp as the outfitter's single-engine aircraft rises off the runway. The plane's tethering shadow drops behind, diminishes, blurs, disappears. We float free. I cherish this grandiose view from the air that puts everything together. Never do I feel such affection for, nor feel so tied to, this patterned earth as when I fly above it, anchored by a gravity of the heart and a river going south while I go north.

We cross over the dark purple brown Mancos Shale badlands that blanket the midsection of eastern Utah like a horizontal "S." This shale doesn't crumble, even along the deep gullies, but instead, holds its shape in smooth, rounded cleavages. The soft voluptuous forms of the easily eroded shale give way to the knife-edged formations of the Mesa Verde Group that make up the Book Cliffs. Tan boulders, fallen from the cap rock, jam the gullies below. The plane veers east, and, nose pressed to the window, I watch the scallops and tiers of slopes disappear under a talus fall, reappear around a corner, a landscape of infinite logic, crisply contoured, an intricate juxtaposition of sandstone and shale—and not a road in sight.

Gray Canyon cuts through the Mesa Verde Group; Desolation Canyon, through the Wasatch and Green River Formations. Sixty to sixty-five million years ago, the silts that became the Green River Formation sifted down into huge, shallow Lake Uinta, which covered a large part of Utah. On the fluctuating shoreline of the lake's edge, as it expanded and contracted, the sandstones and siltstones of the Wasatch Formation were laid, and there the lake and shoreline formations intertongue. We now fly over big cliffs of the Wasatch, sharp and blocky, notched, limned with salt between layers of tan and red brown. In the river, their reflections glow a warm copper, the river fabric blurred like warp-dyed silk.

And then we enter the Green River Basin, and the pallid Green River Formation stretches as far as I can see, subtle grays and sagebrush greens, cream, ash, capped by pale gray sandstones. The discrete ribbons of color and the fine, even layers phase in and out in extraordinary harmony.

The plane bumps to a stop on top of the plateau, a landing strip paved only with big sagebrush and matchweed. As we walk down to the river, we traverse the slopes of the Green River Formation, and what was visible from the air becomes tactile on the ground: shale so finely layered that it resembles pages in a book. Every ashy-white slab, although it looks tightly compressed, flakes apart easily, splitting with the release of pressure into paper-thin sheets, revealing the rich, dark chocolate brown of oil shale. The fine sediments that make up this shale sifted so slowly into ancient Lake Uinta that dark narrow laminae of fall and winter contrast with the lighter, wider layers of spring and summer.

Waiting at the edge of the river is an assortment of rafts, inflated kayaks, and one Sportyak. Once on the river, the harmony of the landscape coalesces into the pleasurable rhythm of rowing. The oarlocks wheeze softly, water drips silkily off the oar blades. I lean forward and pull back, breathe into the motion until it becomes automatic. A light breeze fingers the nape of my neck. My mind floats free. Such is the intense detachment, the easy rhythm, the sybaritic enjoyment, that my thoughts are of reflections and sounds, sediments and centuries. Backlighting intensifies the color of the box elder trees along the shore, an acid green saturated with yellow, the only bright hue in this otherwise subdued landscape. Intellectually, I know there are boats behind and in front of me, but I see no one. I feel as alone as I wish to be, on this painted river with wavelets dancing upstream, against the grain, running backwards into yesterday.

A stately grebe paddles in an eddy, dives, reappears, proceeds in leisurely fashion. Two unidentified sandpipers take off, flutter and glide, alight, repeat, going downstream ahead of me. On shore, ubiquitous grasshoppers lob up out of the grass, spreading dark brown wings edged in cream. Silent, without the usual grasshopper clacking, they look more like mourning cloak butterflies than grasshoppers.

A damselfly with dark wings and body, an elegant red smudge at the base of its wings, alights on the oarshaft. I've seen it only in entomology book illustrations, and the gift of its presence pleases me inordinately. I anticipate reading about it, finding and typing out its name—*Hataerina americana,* or ruby spot—a name that gives me access to another piece of the continually fascinating puzzle of the natural world. It is all the more delightful because it is the only ruby spot I see. The other damselflies are the common bluets, chalky blue bodies hyphenating the river bank. Most are locked in the "P" of mating flight, a single-letter alphabet repeated above the water, among the willows, and on the gunwales of the boat, guaranteeing next year's population of damselflies.

Coming up the canyon from another direction, I might not have seen them, a few rocks that look like all the other random rocks around, but juxtaposed in an order that spells man's hand. Between 700 and 1250 A.D., a prehistoric people called the Fremont Anasazi walked the prickled paths of Utah, Arizona, and New Mexico. Separated by space far enough and long enough, they developed living patterns slightly different from other Anasazi groups, yet generically similar enough that they clearly shared a common heritage, imprinted by the necessities of a stern environment. They colonized eastern Utah, up and down the Green and Fremont River drainages. Like the Anasazi to the south, they cultivated corn and beans and probably squash, but they never lost their knowledge of the plants and animals that stocked the countryside, never lost that vision of what was ripe where and when, and if not, where to go to find what was. Depending on your perspective, they were semisedentary nomads, or seminomadic agriculturists.

The Fremont fashioned magnificent baskets, finely made and tightly woven: conical baskets that fit on their backs, in which they carried plants and grain; flat winnowing baskets, on which they shook seeds so the husks could float on the wind; toasting baskets, in which they tumbled with hot stones the seeds they had taken days to gather; and fat baskets resembling pots, in which, when waterproofed with pitch, they heated water by dropping in sizzling stones. They also fashioned ingenious sandals out of bighorn sheep hide, placing the dewclaw just under the heel to neatly form a cleat.

The shards of their simple pottery turn up along the river, a grayware made of local clays, tempered with ground-up rock or pulverized shards to keep it from cracking, every piece carefully smoothed and slipped on the inside. On the outside, the regular pinching and crimping that united the coils was left as a corrugated pattern, a roughness that made a big pot easier to grasp and to carry.

The Fremont lived in caves or built simple shelters—this one probably unroofed, perhaps no more than a windbreak, or a place to process grain and seeds. Built forty feet up off the valley floor, the view from here looks both ways, up the deepening shadowy green canyon, down across the flats to the river. This place was a home, this notched horizon familiar, these rough walls expected, these slopes imprinted on the memory. Here was where you went for rice grass; there, the best prickly pear fruit was to be found at the end of summer; yonder, the bighorns came to water and could be felled; and here, I can stretch out muscles, shut my eyes and dream of ancient faces that look out from mysterious pictographs, eternal on their sandstone walls.

Another day. We noon just above Duchess Hole. The sun is heavy; the sand, warm. I dine on a lettuce-and-tomato-and-lethargy sandwich for lunch. Across the river, the repeated orderly bays of the Green River Formation cliffs and their impeccably corresponding shadows look drawn by a draftsman's hand. The big red sandstones of the Wasatch Formation are painted with a broad, impressionistic brush; those of the Green River, precise, lined with pale ink.

During lunch, the breeze has steadily stiffened into a dedicated wind. We decide to remain a couple of hours longer in the fervent hope that it will slacken or, better, go away. The afternoon drags on. The wind works itself up to gusting blue tantrums. Finally there is no choice but to go on downriver, and no more reluctant body ever folded itself into a boat.

The wind traps me to shore. With stubborn determination, I dig the oars in, and it feels as if I bury them in cement. I plow out ten feet, get smacked back into shore. I key on a branch stuck in the beach. The wind shoves me past it, going upstream—three times.

In a blessed lull, I gain enough ground to get unplastered from the beach, just in time to set up for a big riffle. I run it head-on with no grace, almost blinded with spray that hurls off the oars, dashes stinging splinters of glass into my face. I spin around to get my back to the wind, and gusts from shore sandblast my hands. I brace into rowing long, hard, measured strokes. The wind is strong enough to affect the current itself; not only do the surface wavelets break upstream but the current of the river beneath follows. When the gusts intensify, I ship the oars, hunch over and use those minutes to list the pains of flesh and heart I will no longer be heir to: if I can survive this wind, I can survive anything. A lull comes, I pick up the cadence, regain what I lost and a yard more. This insufferable wind may have helped sculpt these magnificent cliffs, but, thankfully, I do not have to withstand a few millennia of its misery. This wind makes mortality look good.

I row on. Days pass. I stretch into each stroke. Months pass. At the turn of the New Year I see boats pulled over downriver. A decade later, I pull into shore and creak out of the boat like a spavined spider. My fingers will not straighten but remain neatly curved to the haft of the handle. My knees are the reverse: they won't bend.

The wind gnashes its teeth and beats its breast long after dark, and the conversation invariably turns to wilderness: if it is so difficult, if we are so beset, why are we here? I suppose there may be as many answers to "What is wilderness?" and "Why go?" as there are people asked. We know what it isn't, but we're not sure what it is, although we think we know it when we see it.

The most frequent response is along the lines of "wilderness is the place I go to get away from stress and the confusions of city and job or family problems, get my head together, look inside and find myself." I puzzle these answers, print them off in my head, collate and staple, and try to make sense of a definition at variance with my own.

I get my head together sitting at the computer, doing research, making salad, being apart of a prescribed world. I go to the wilderness to get *un*together, and I prefer to go alone. Wilderness is being totally responsible for one's well-being, without the social and mechanical crutches of everyday life. I go to focus outward; to observe as astutely as possible, to learn, to become a giant sponge, soaking up everything, making a list of the answers for the questions I do not yet know,

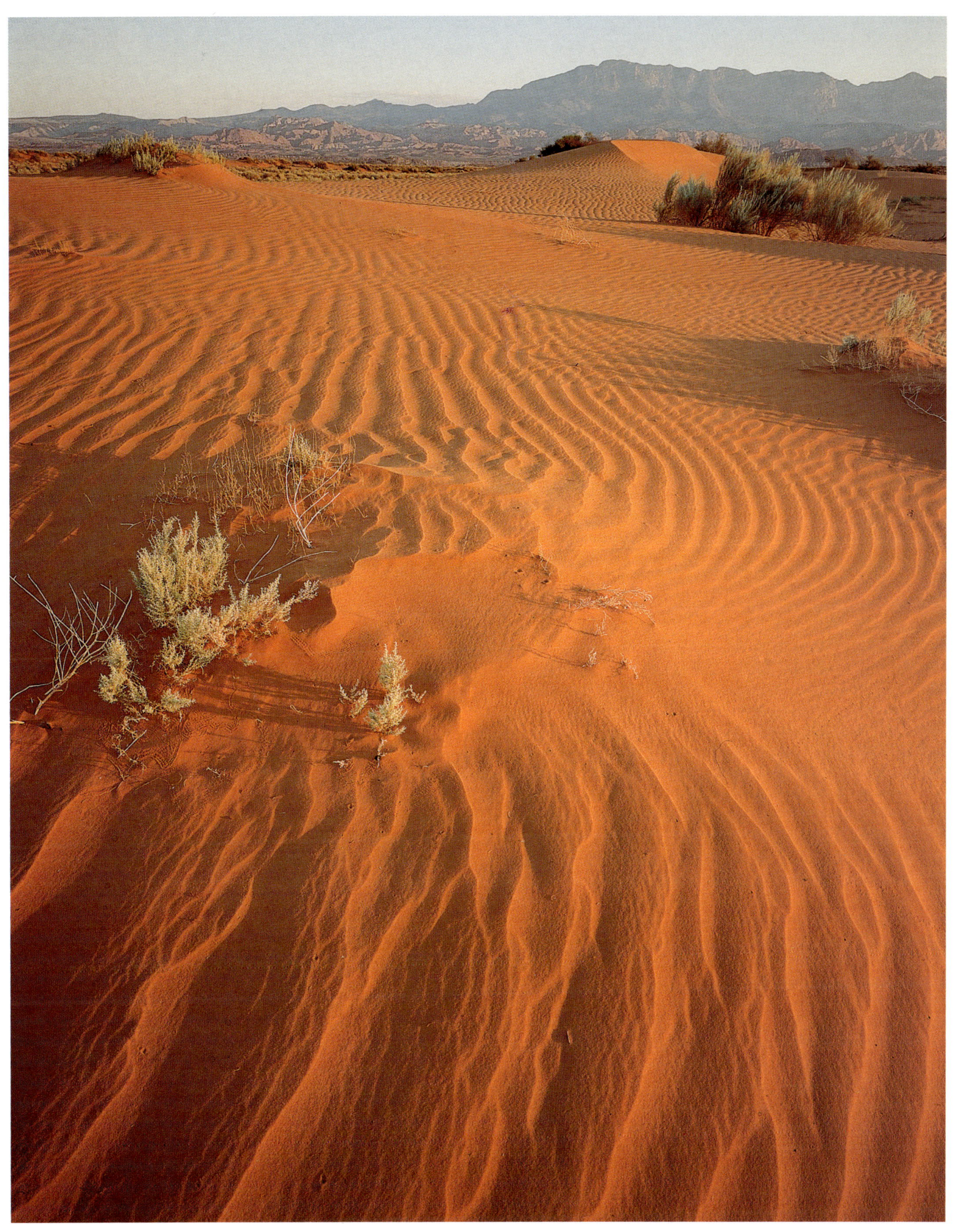

RED SANDS OF WARNER VALLEY WITH PINE VALLEY MOUNTAINS, DIXIE CORRIDOR NEAR SAINT GEORGE.

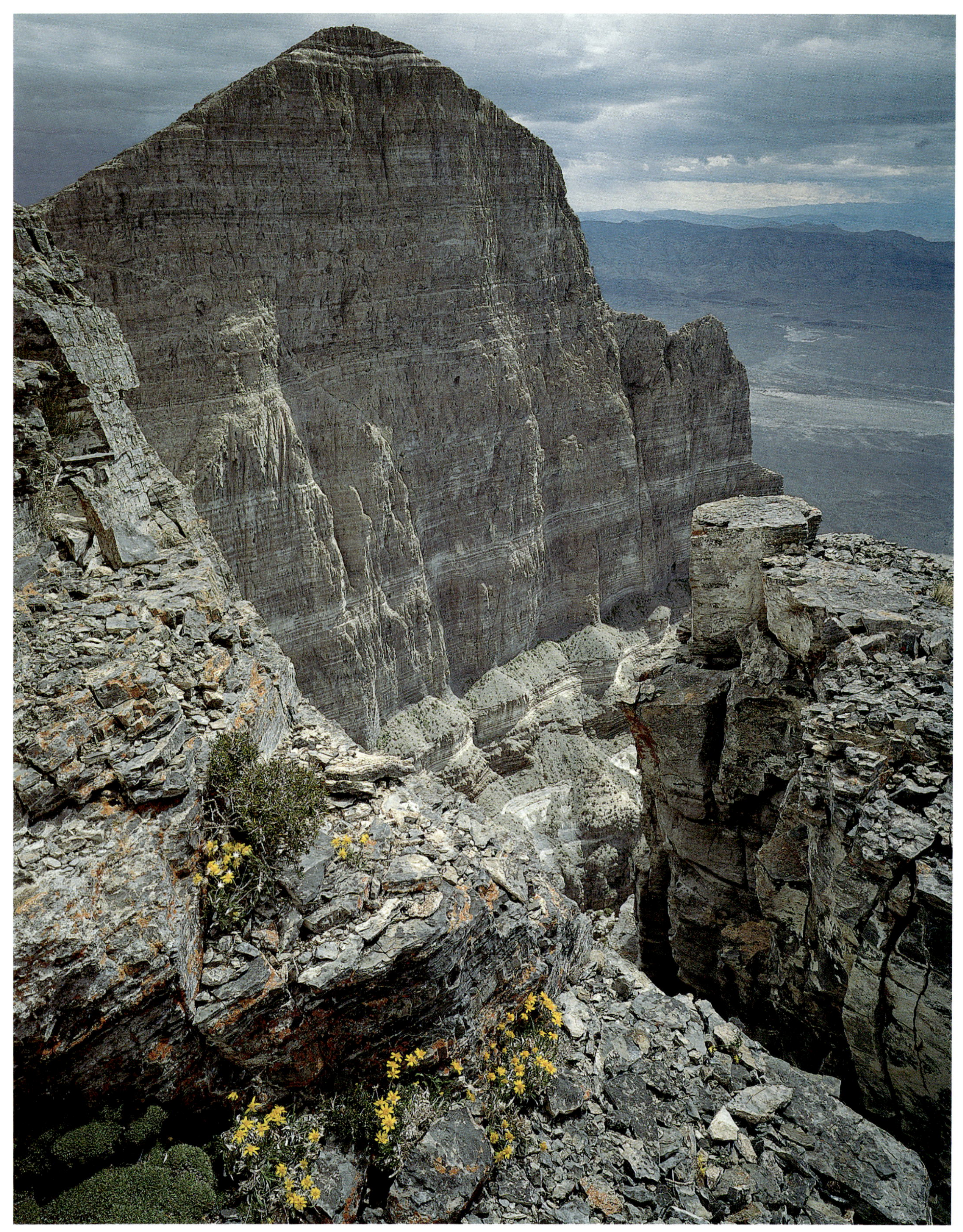

2,800-FOOT LIMESTONE WALL ON THE NORTH FACE OF NOTCH PEAK, HOUSE RANGE.

reaching into the wilderness of the intellect. I go to listen as keenly as the kangaroo rat, to smell as sharply as the whiptail lizard, to be as aware of touch as the scorpion, to watch the inner workings and the outer goings-on of a beautifully running natural world. I go to be slightly off-balance, as wary as the hunted, as vigilant as the hunter, to court change, perceive other realities, edit what I am thinking, be precise about how I am living. And if I am lucky, I am absorbed into that natural world, the silent watcher, dissolving into sunshine.

Nature writing is my avocation. Gathering river rocks is my profession. River rocks tend to be slightly flatter than ocean cobbles, and there may be, if you look long enough, just another half mile down the beach, the perfect river rock. Picking up river rocks is meditation, slowing the brain waves to serenity. A river rock in the hand injects quietude directly through the lifeline into the bloodstream.

This morning I scuffle along the beach between Wire Fence Rapid and Three Fords, two big rapids within walking distance of each other. Last evening I came over the lip of Wire Fence and looked straight down over a five-foot drop that tailed away in a froth of back wave and a rumble of rollers. The Sportyak bucked and slewed, took a couple buckets of river, and ran neatly down the tail waves.

But Three Fords is something else, the only rapid I've ever flipped in, a sickening memory that comes back with indelible and unbidden clarity. One moment I was upright, squinting against the sun; the next, the world was dark, part of me submerged, part of me breathing air, and the sensations were so at odds with each other and the change so sudden that my whole reaction was one of surprise and bewilderment. Then the overturned boat popped off my head, there was again sunshine and reason and a huge wave breaking toward me. Another surprise: the boat and I simply rode over it, giving me a splendid river's-eye view, the water drops on my eyelashes framing it through hexagons of light.

Today I scuffle the sand thoughtfully, concentrating on how Three Fords looks this year at low water and how I have run it. I flip pebbles with my toes and they fly like stone grasshoppers. I pick up one of dark gray shale, a five-eighths-inch isosceles triangle, thin, with a silky feel. Conversations over the years with others who pick up beach pebbles fade in and out of my mind. I have a friend who chooses rocks by color and stacks them in cairns to choose the best few later; another who picks up cobbles big enough to be manos; a daughter who chooses only the exotic, the colorful, the unusual.

It is the shape that appeals to me. When I have a handful of the most handsome pebbles, I lay them out in a row and discover worlds about this canyon. All are survivors, none over two inches. Sandstone pebbles are fat, plump-but-not-round, pale, rainy, pillowed ovals. The shales are thinner, become smoother. The sandstone pebbles have a gritty jounce in my hand. The shales clink with a soft sibilance. I marvel at the precise way in which the river rounds and ovals and thins, that no matter what their original shape, they have worn to these generic shapes: fat for sandstone, slivered for shale. I count them in my hand, the coin of the beach, the worry beads of the river.

When I have run Three Fords right side up, I choose the three most perfect pebbles and fling them back into the river as alms.

Last night out. Cicadas chirrup away the twilight. The sand is fine and molds into a sumptuous sleeping surface. The temperature on my thermometer slices right at seventy degrees, not an increment above, not an increment below. In the softening darkness a breeze waltzes its way across the dune, indolent and careless; it elbows the dried cottonwoods, braids starlight through my hair, whispers soft quixotic messages into my ears.

The Milky Way wavers across the sky like a pale chiffon scarf, swathing the heavens, willowy, wafty. The stars quiver behind the knitted cottonwood branches, ready to slip sideways. The whole sky trembles as I fall asleep.

The next morning, there are tiny lizards quilting the sand around my sleeping bag. I had planned to be awake most of the night, unwilling to miss the heavens pivoting by, the stars clicking on and off. Stretched out on elysian sand that cupped to my body, beneath a quivering sky that shot shimmering arrows into the dawn, I slept so soundly that I missed the mincing nuzzlers with the tiny tentative toenails that ticked so close.

I snuggle deeper in my sleeping bag, half-awake in the half-light of morning, and reflect on the necessity of places you can't get to from here, that are available only if you're willing to carry your weight in water or row your way far downstream or march countless miles, only if you're willing to risk your precious identity and stay reminded that the sun always comes up on some segment of the eastern sky and goes down in some segment of western. My years in this Utah wilderness have shaped my thought patterns in mysterious ways: I am no longer embarrassed to speak out loud to stars or animals or to converse courteously with plants, waiting patiently for their pansophic answers; I can forget the days of the week and not even bother to write them in the sand, knowing the wind is infinitely more forgetful than even I am.

Wilderness dictates its own trade-offs. It rearranges mind-sets and ways of reading landscapes, dictates how you unroll your sleeping bag, affects friendships and the ability to go home again, and confounds the way you tie up your boots. It laces my mind with ancient memories of a time when there was only sand and only wind to erase my footprints before I wake.

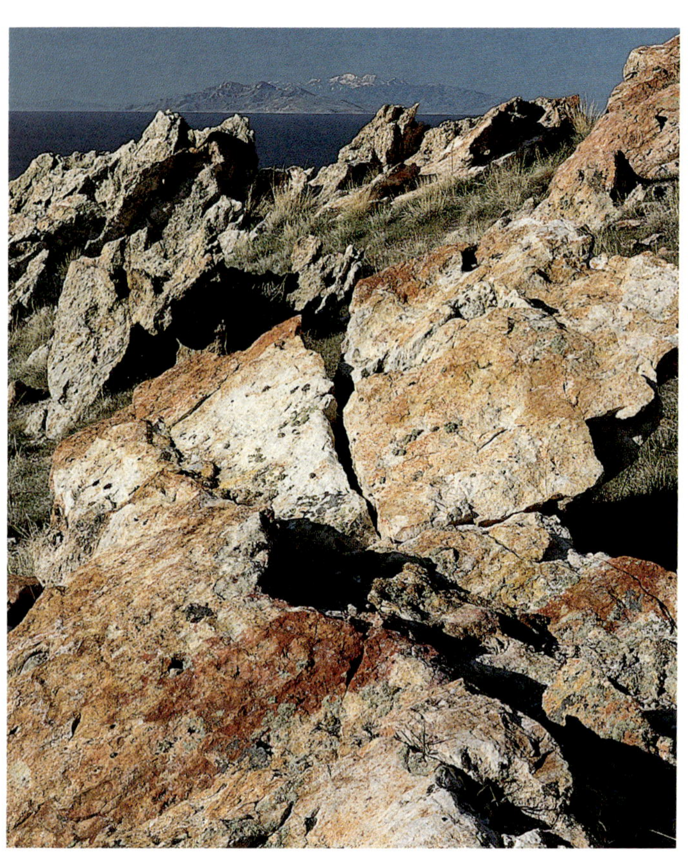

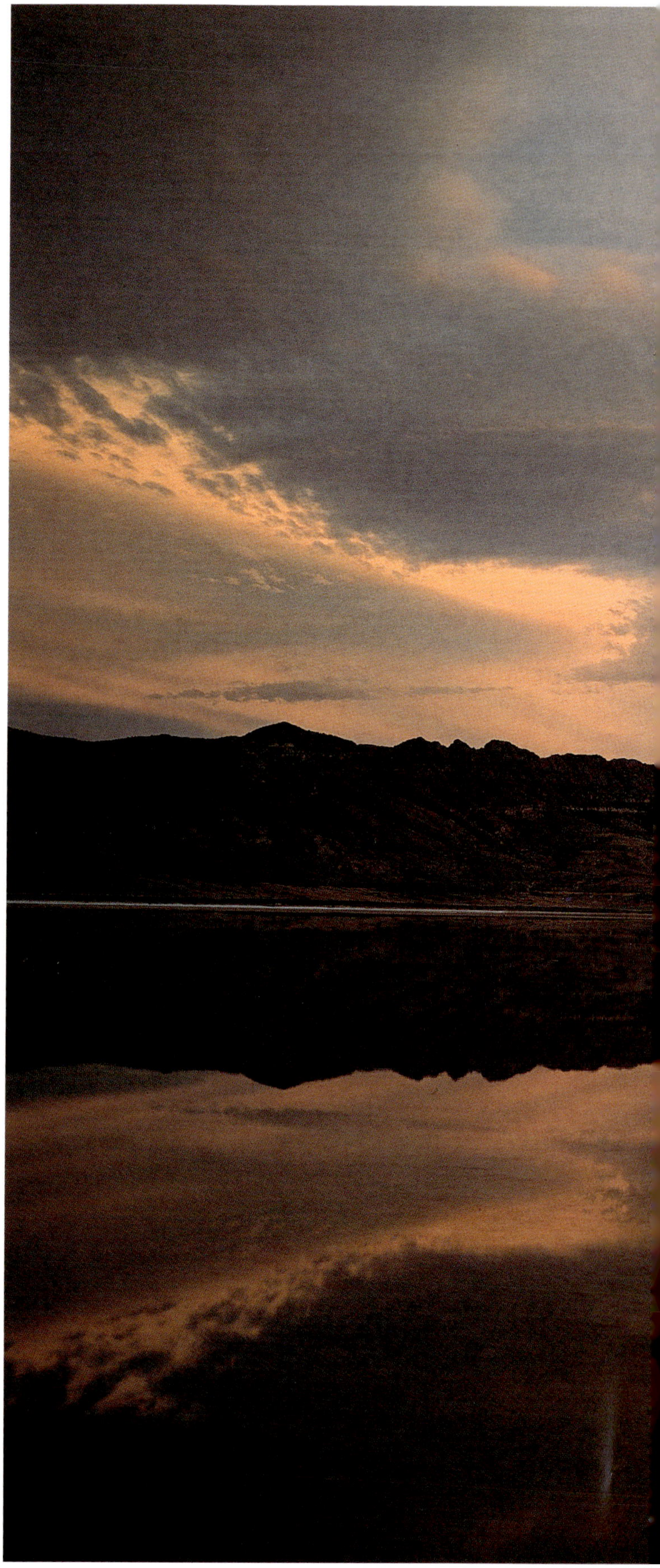

ABOVE: PROMONTORY POINT, GREAT SALT LAKE.

RIGHT: SUMMER EVENING REFLECTION ALONG THE EAST SIDE OF THE STANSBURY MOUNTAINS, GREAT SALT LAKE.

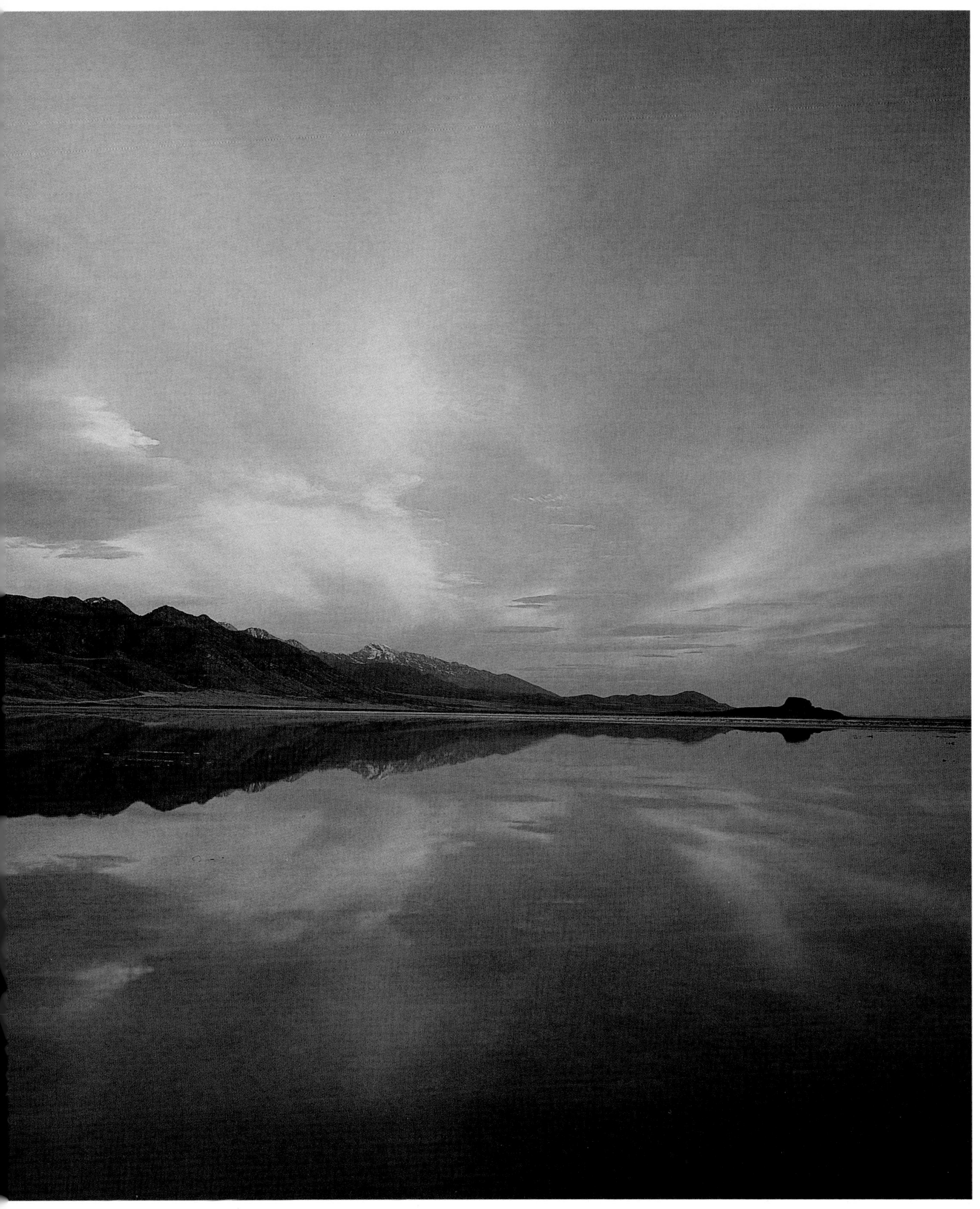

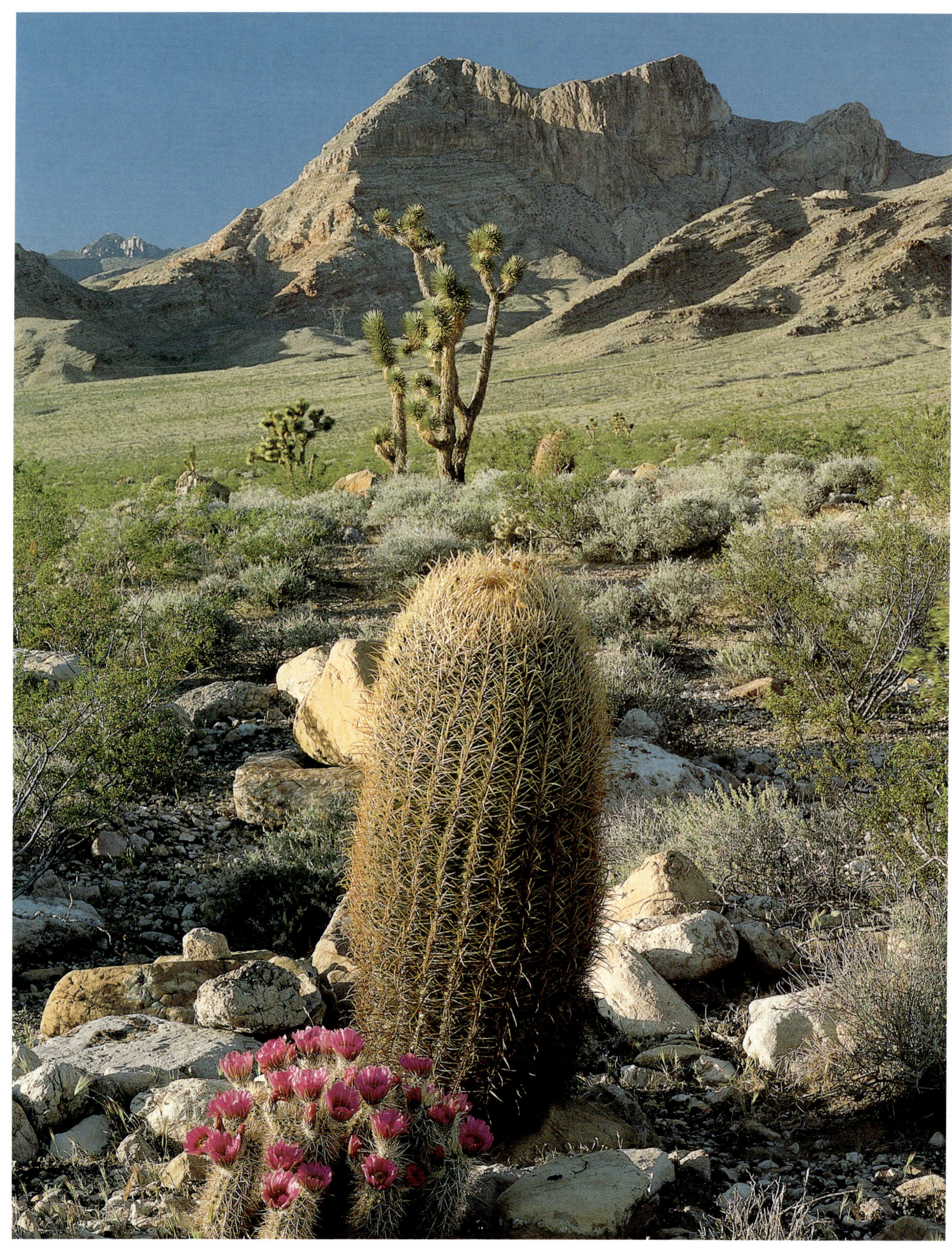

HEDGEHOG AND BARREL CACTUS WITH JOSHUA TREES, BEAVER DAM MOUNTAINS.

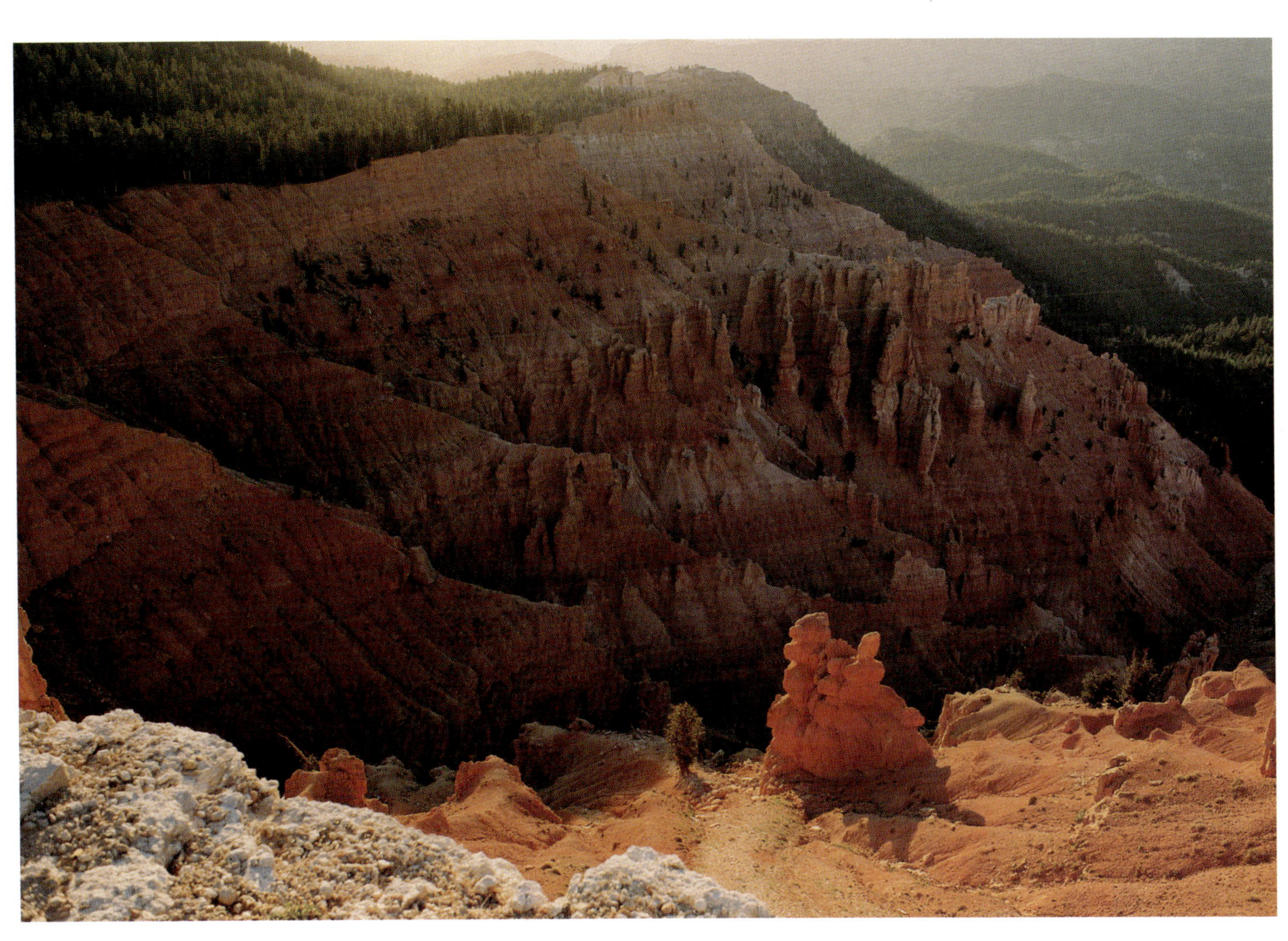

SPECTRA POINT, CEDAR BREAKS.

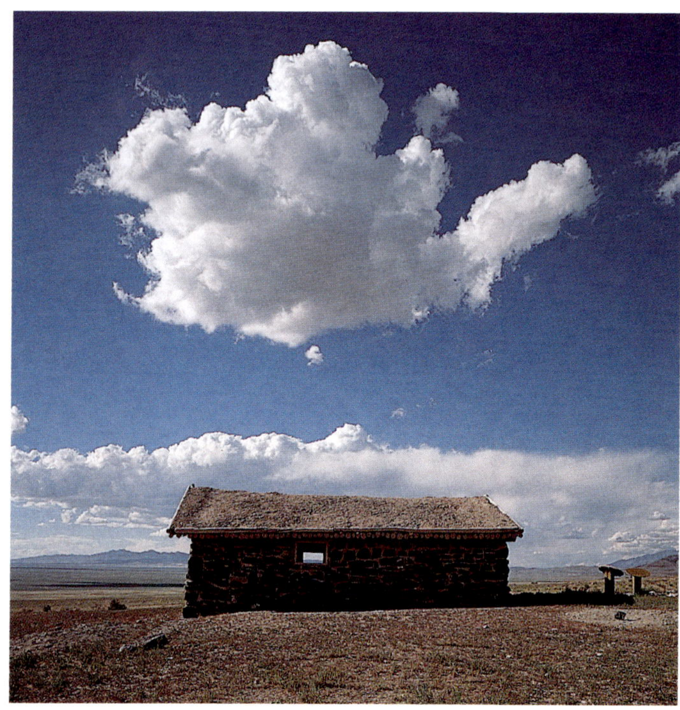

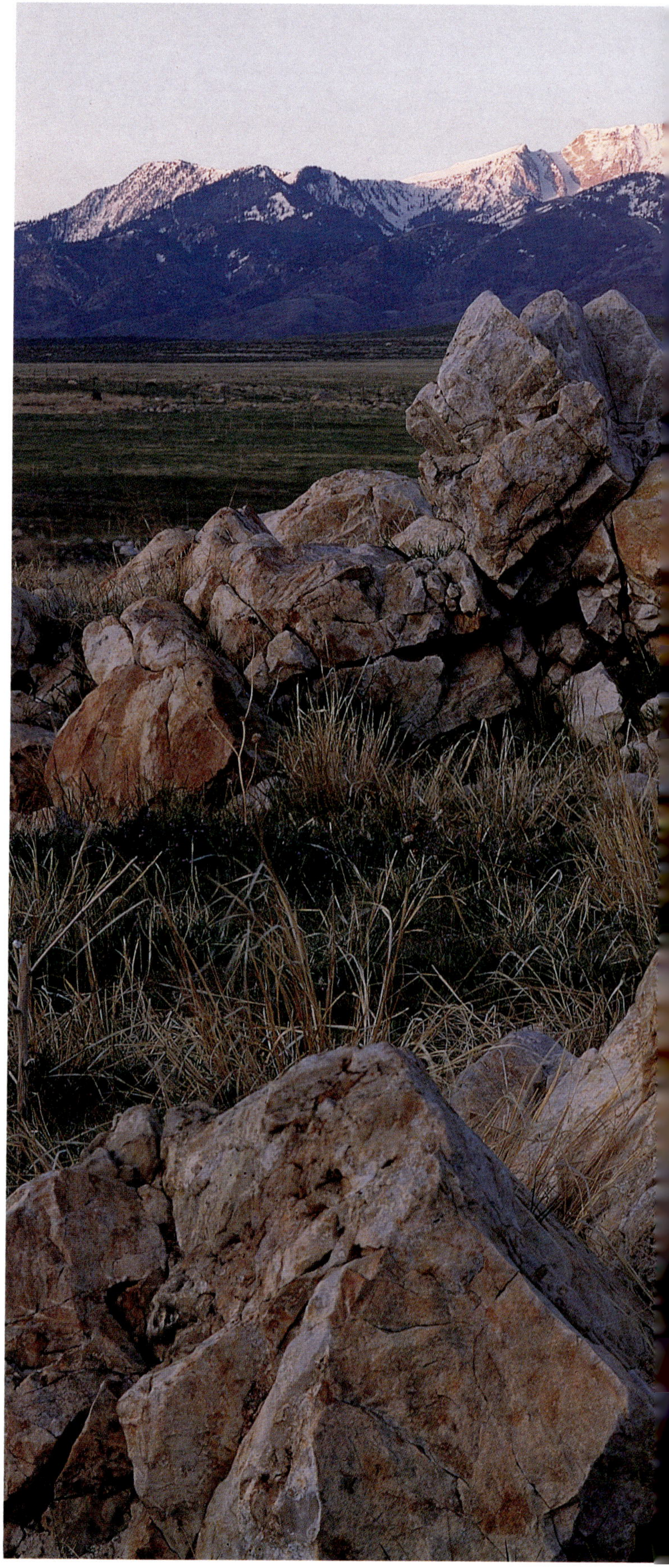

ABOVE: SIMPSON SPRINGS, PONY EXPRESS STATION IN DUGWAY VALLEY, TOOELE COUNTY.

RIGHT: QUARTZITE ROCKS AND DESERET PEAK IN TOOELE VALLEY.

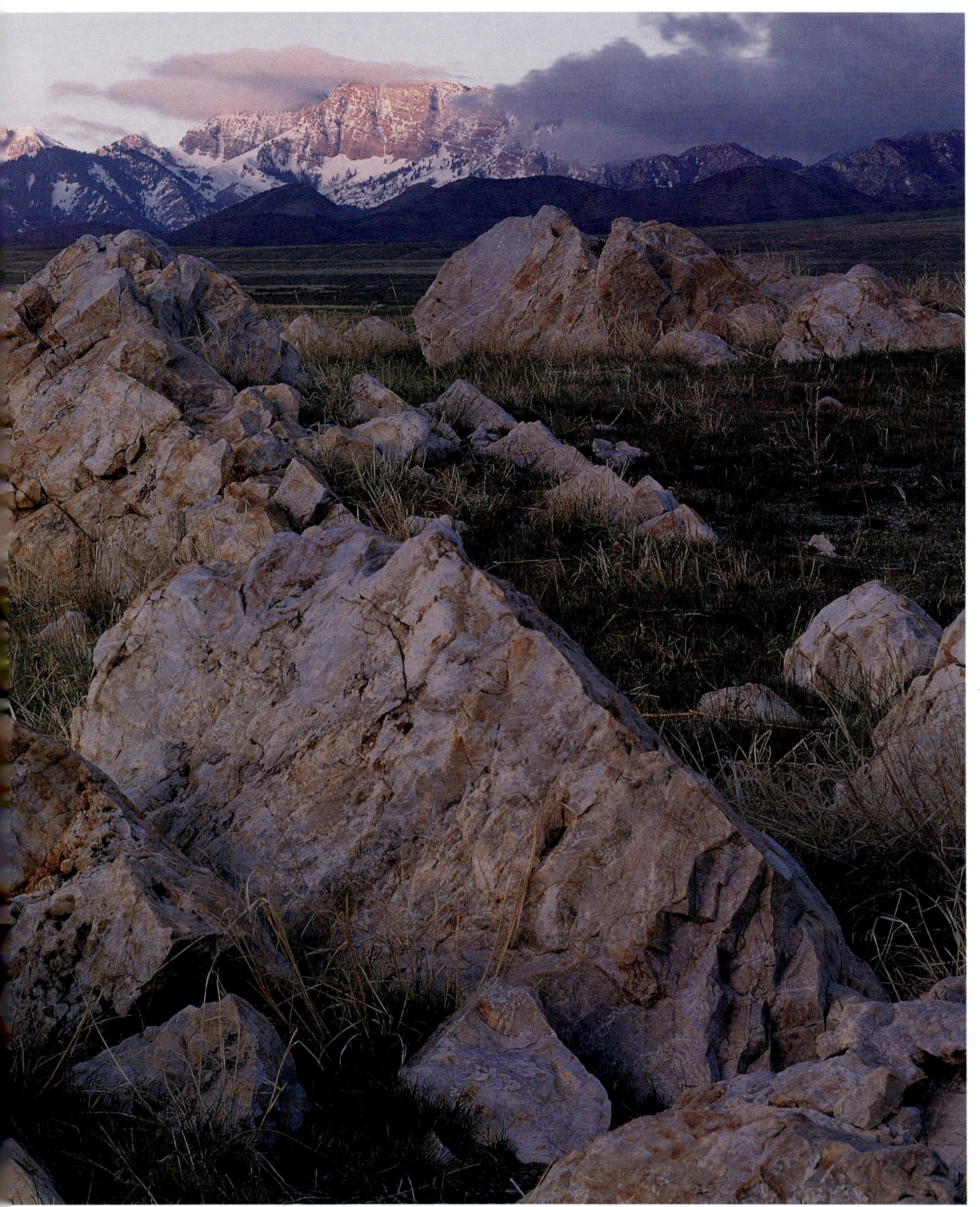

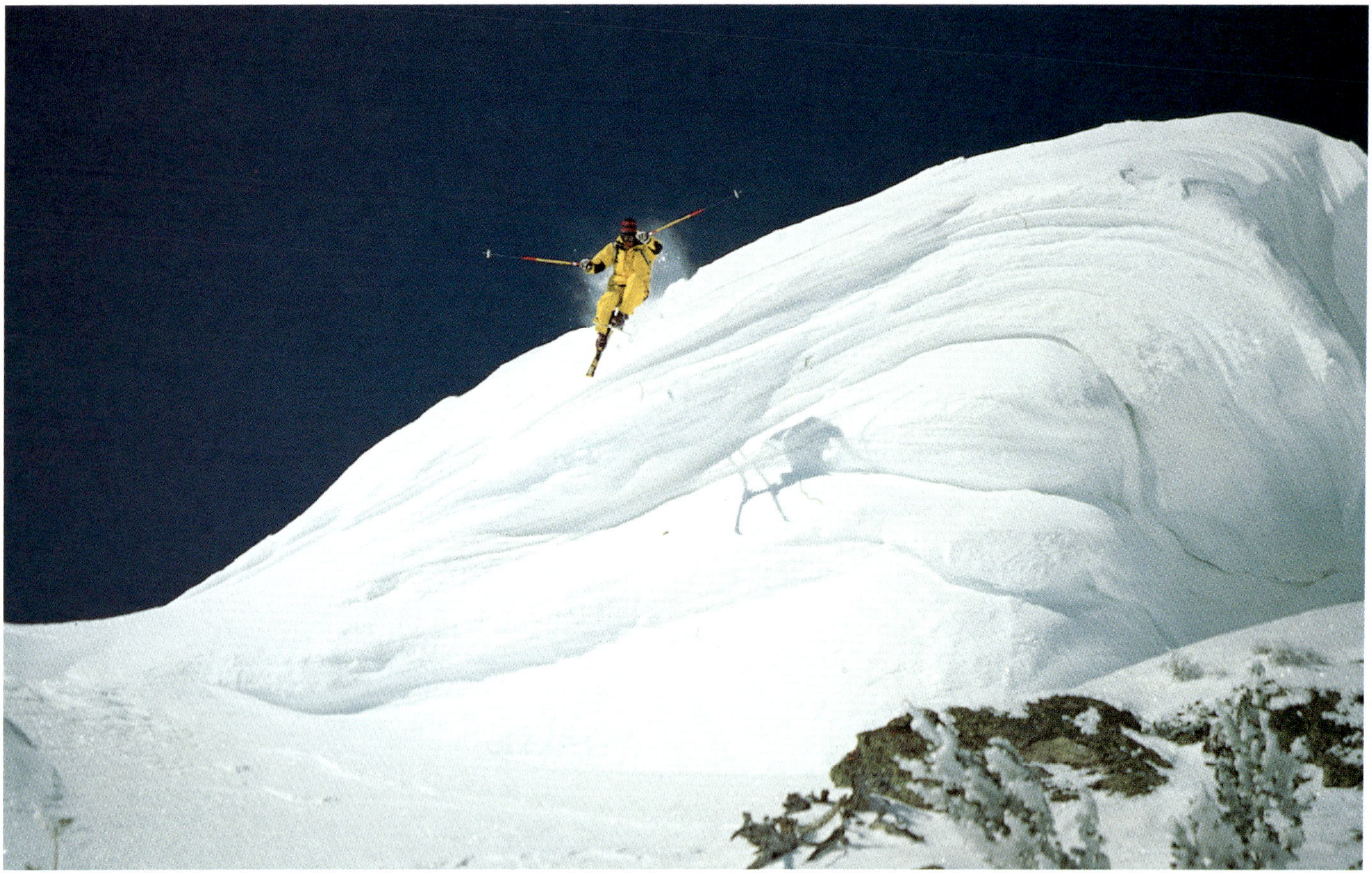

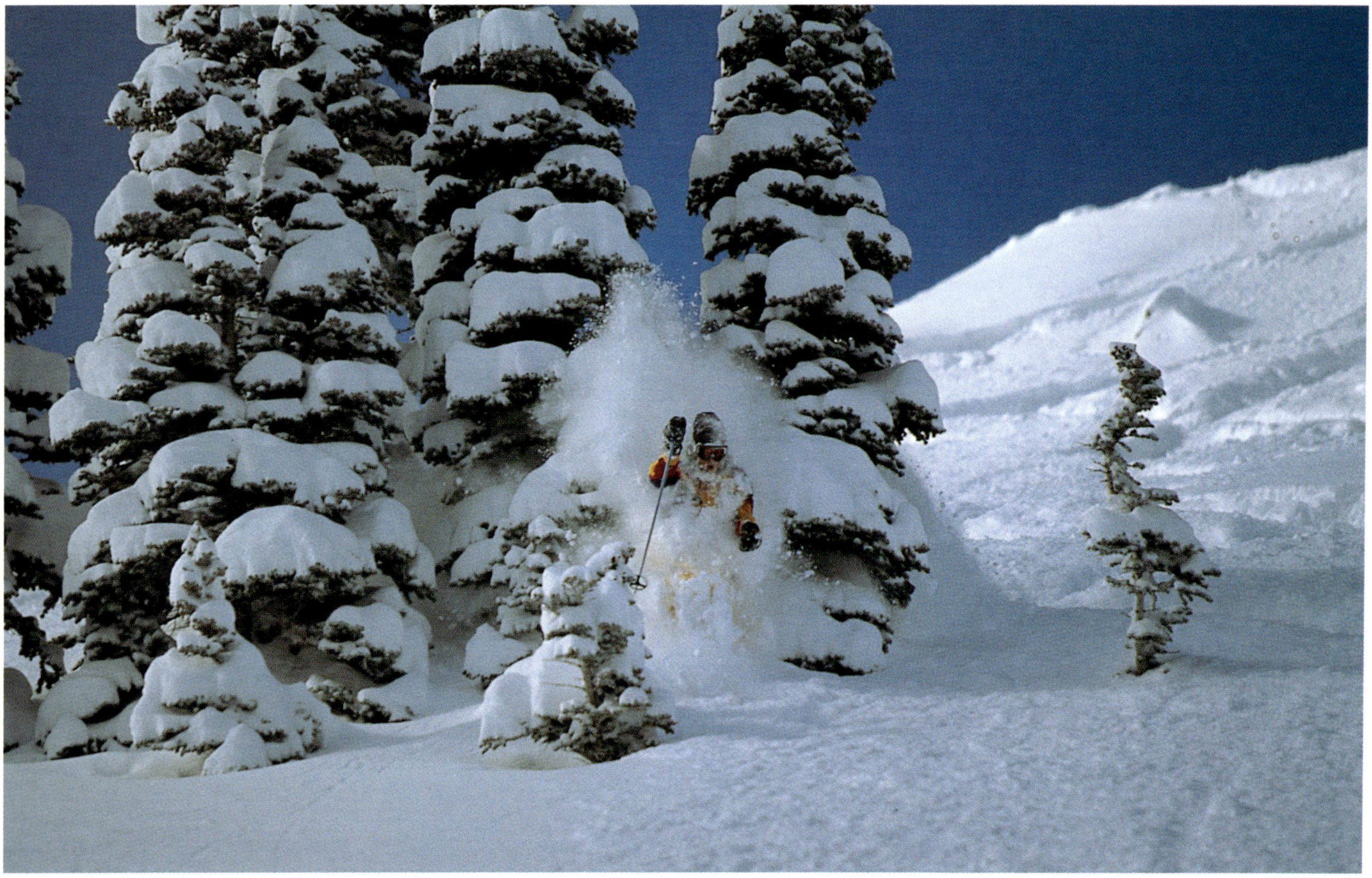

TOP: SNOW BASIN. *BOTTOM:* PERUVIAN CIRQUE, SNOWBIRD. *RIGHT:* WINTER CAMP, TOP OF THE WASATCH RANGE, TWIN PEAKS WILDERNESS.

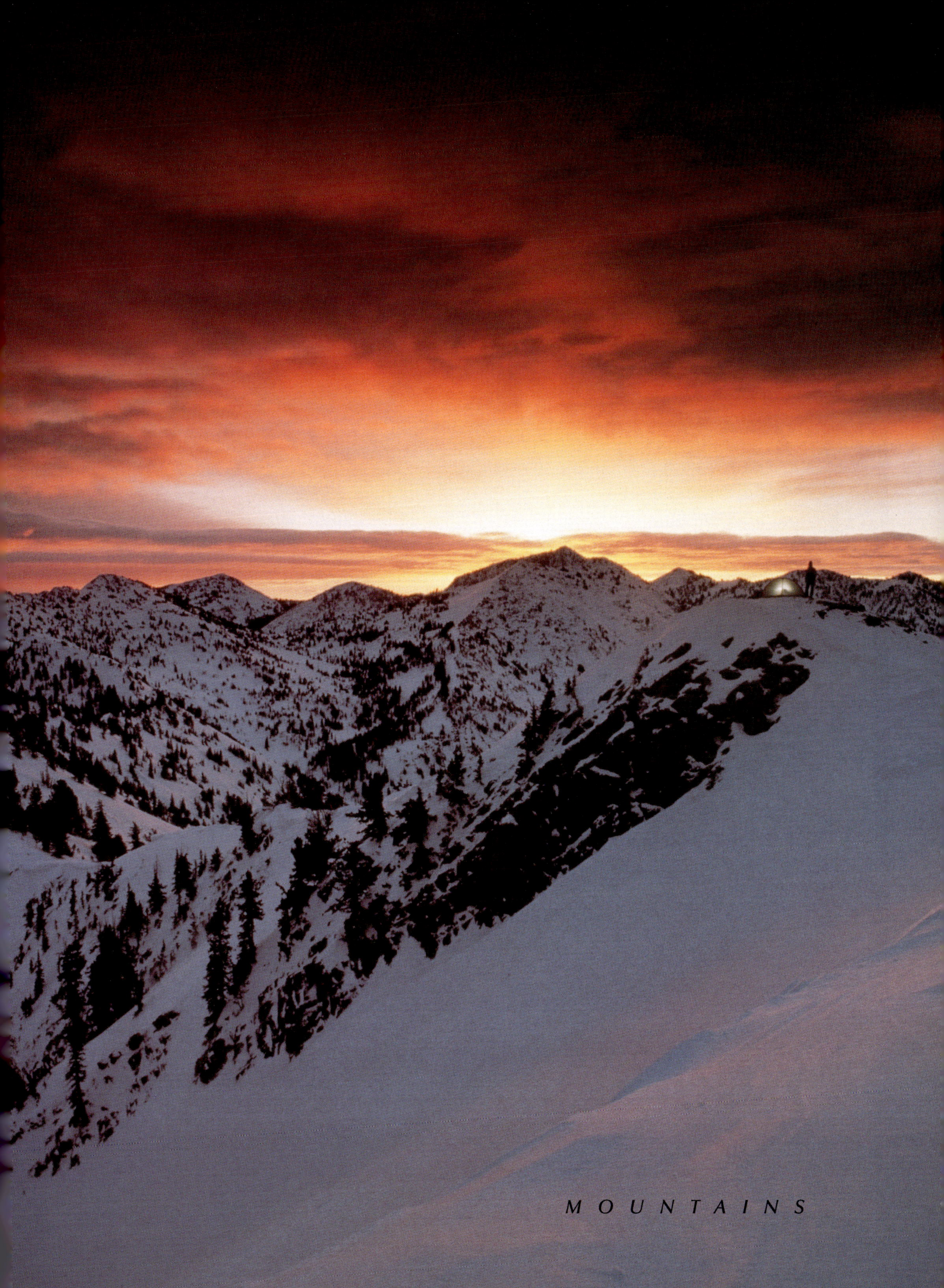

MOUNTAINS

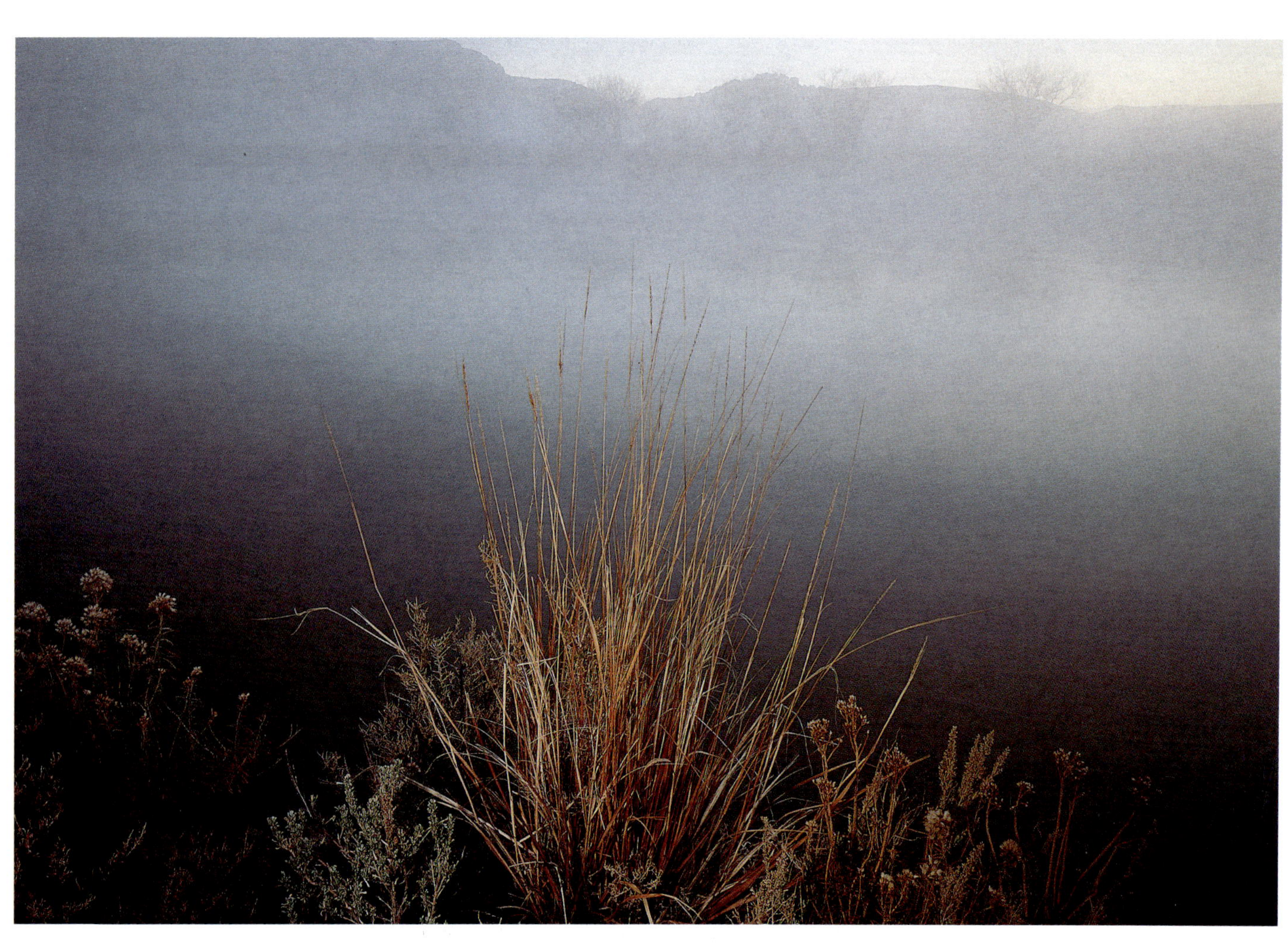

GREEN RIVER EMERGES FROM SPLIT MOUNTAIN, DINOSAUR NATIONAL MONUMENT.

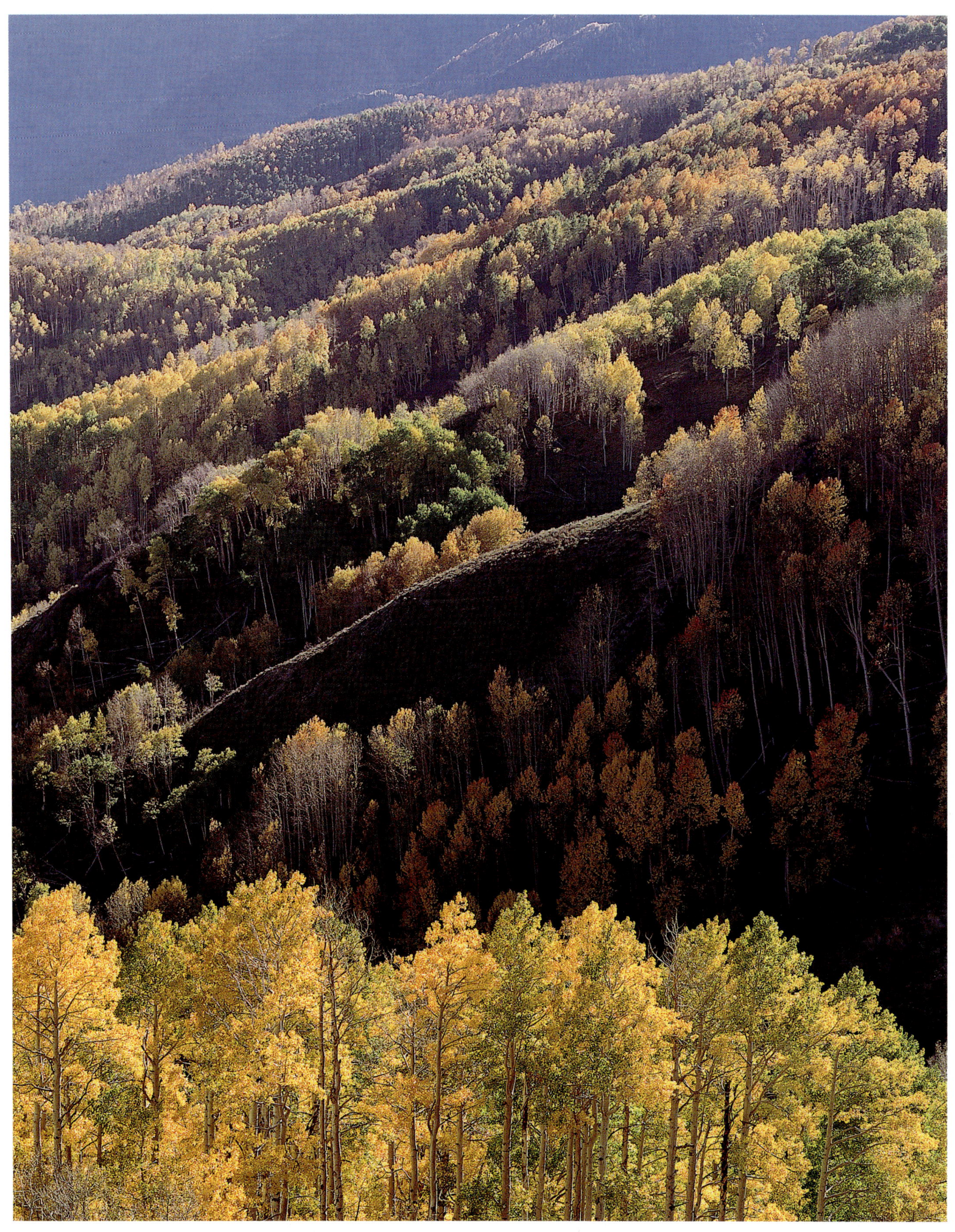

ASPEN IN OCTOBER, MOUNT NEBO WILDERNESS, WASATCH RANGE.

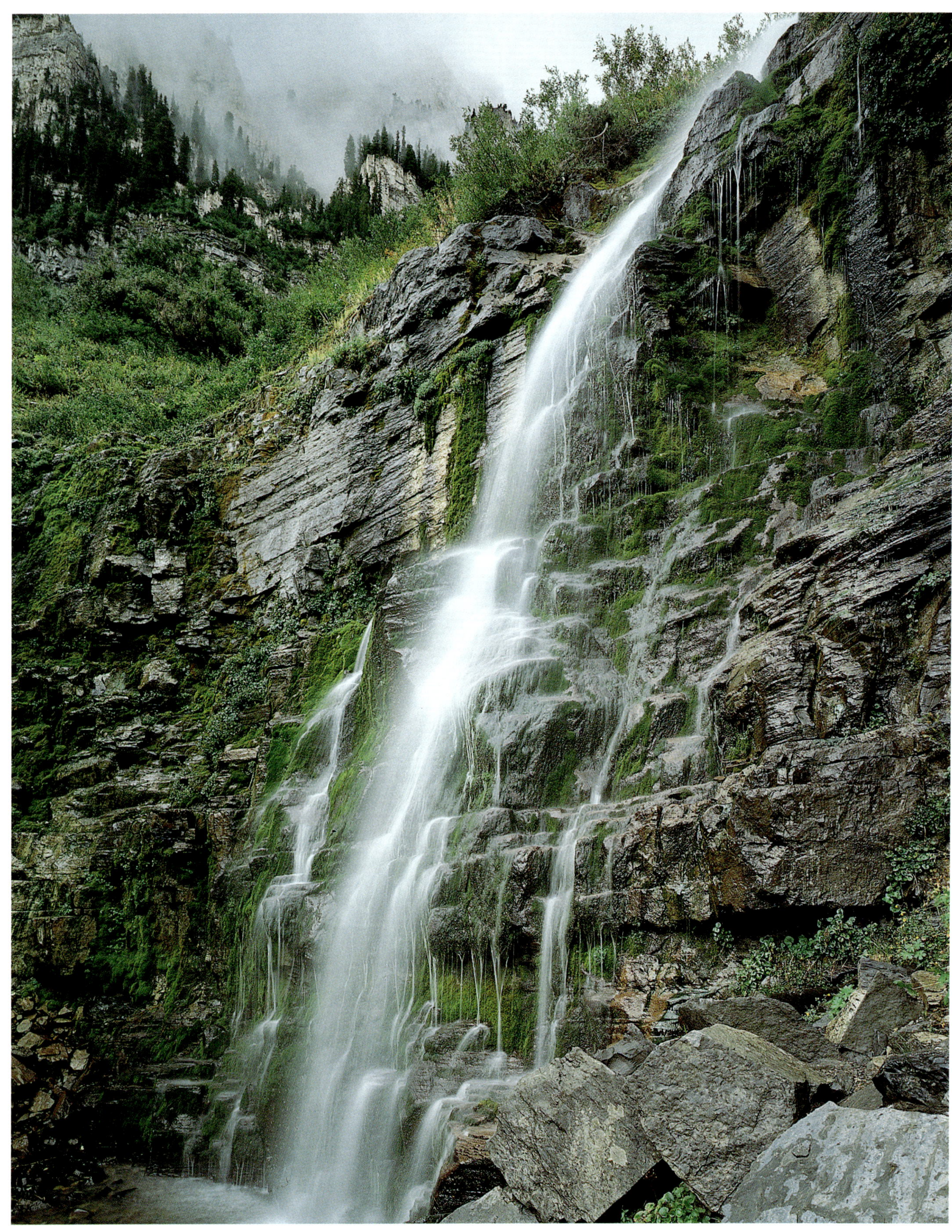

EXPOSED CASCADE WALL ON EAST SIDE OF MOUNT TIMPANOGOS, WASATCH RANGE.

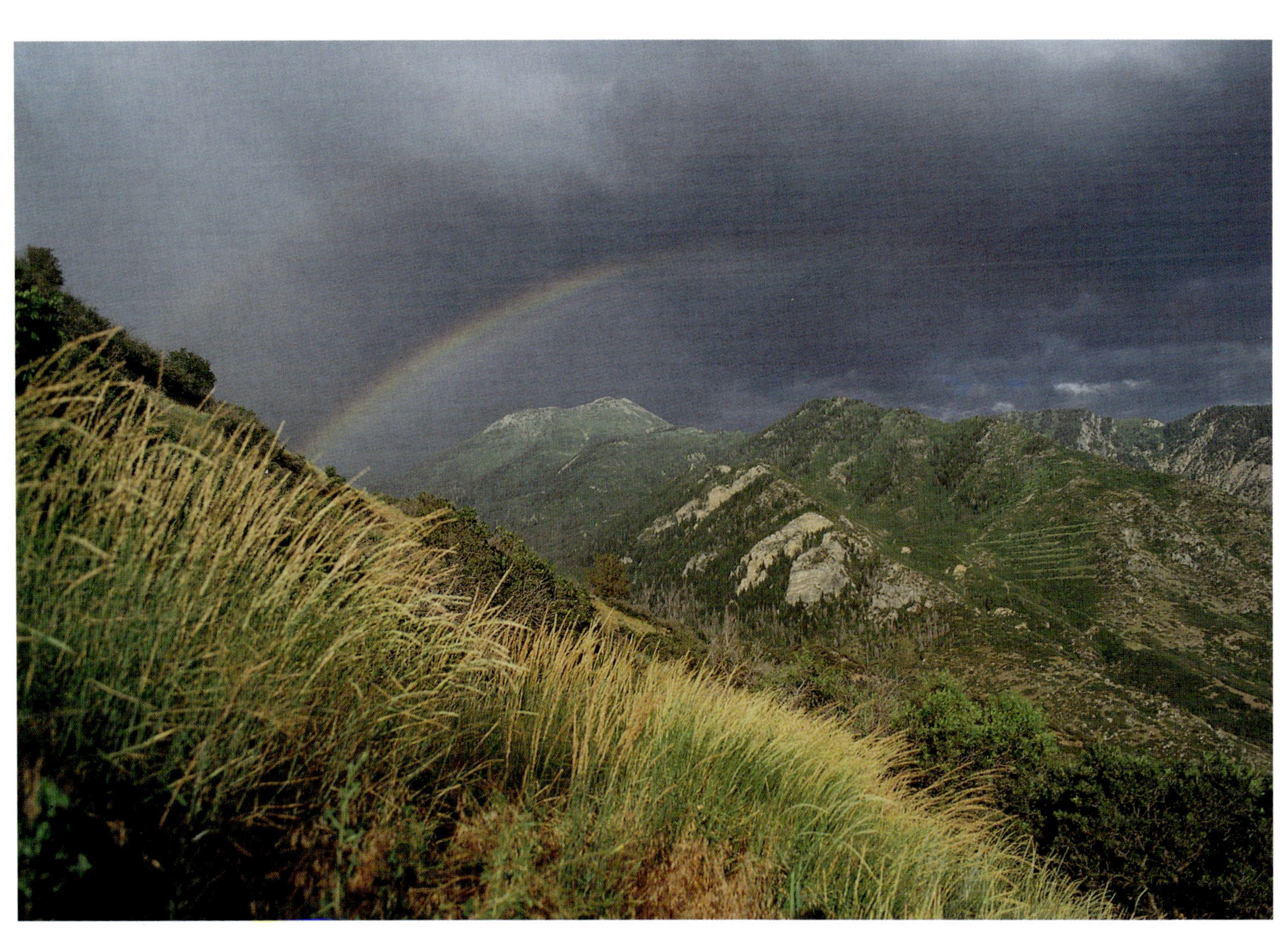

RAINBOW OVER THE WASATCH RANGE.

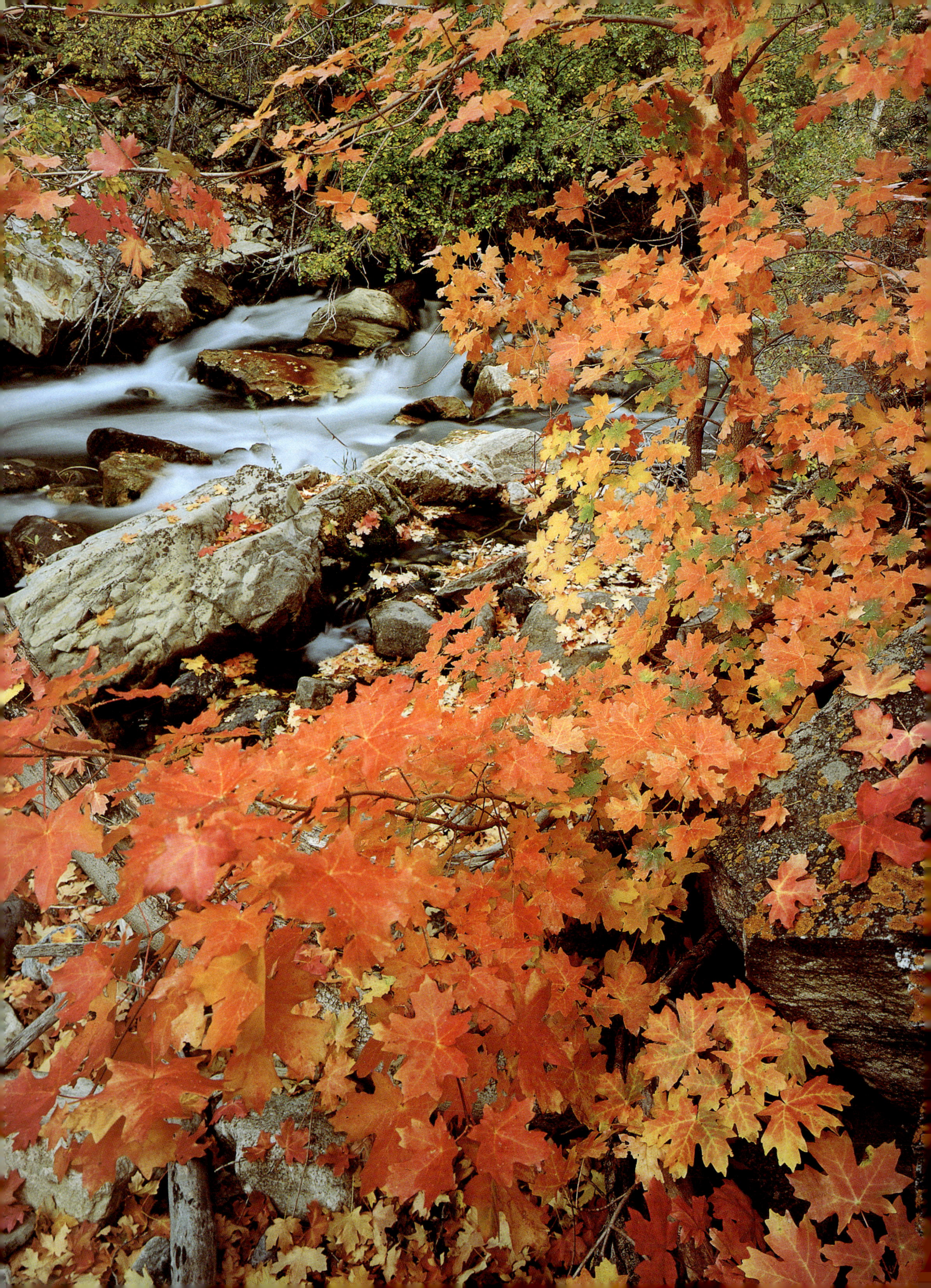

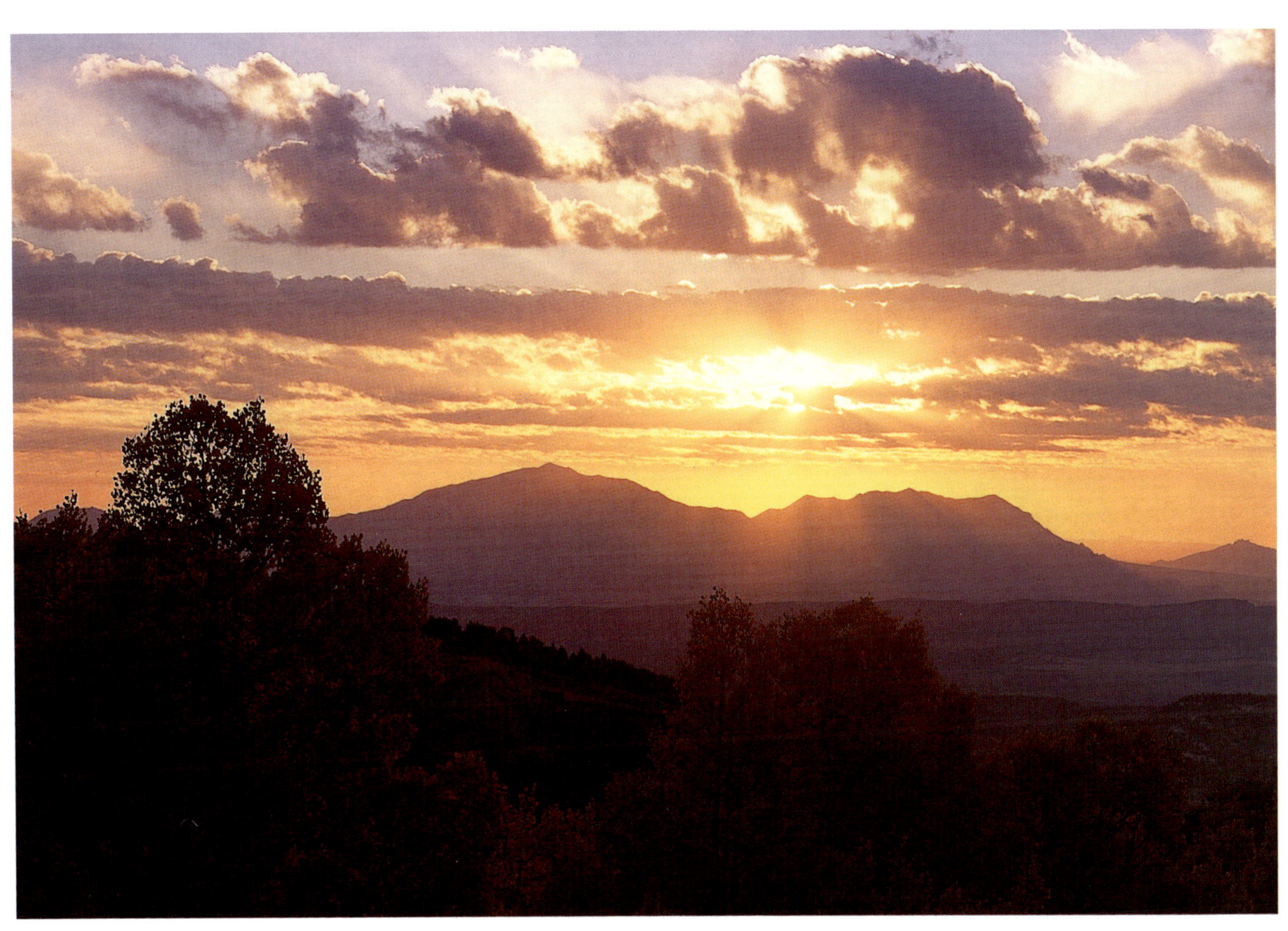

LEFT: BIGTOOTH MAPLE, AMERICAN FORK RIVER CANYON.

ABOVE: AUTUMN ON BOULDER MOUNTAINS

WITH HENRY MOUNTAINS IN THE DISTANT BACKGROUND.

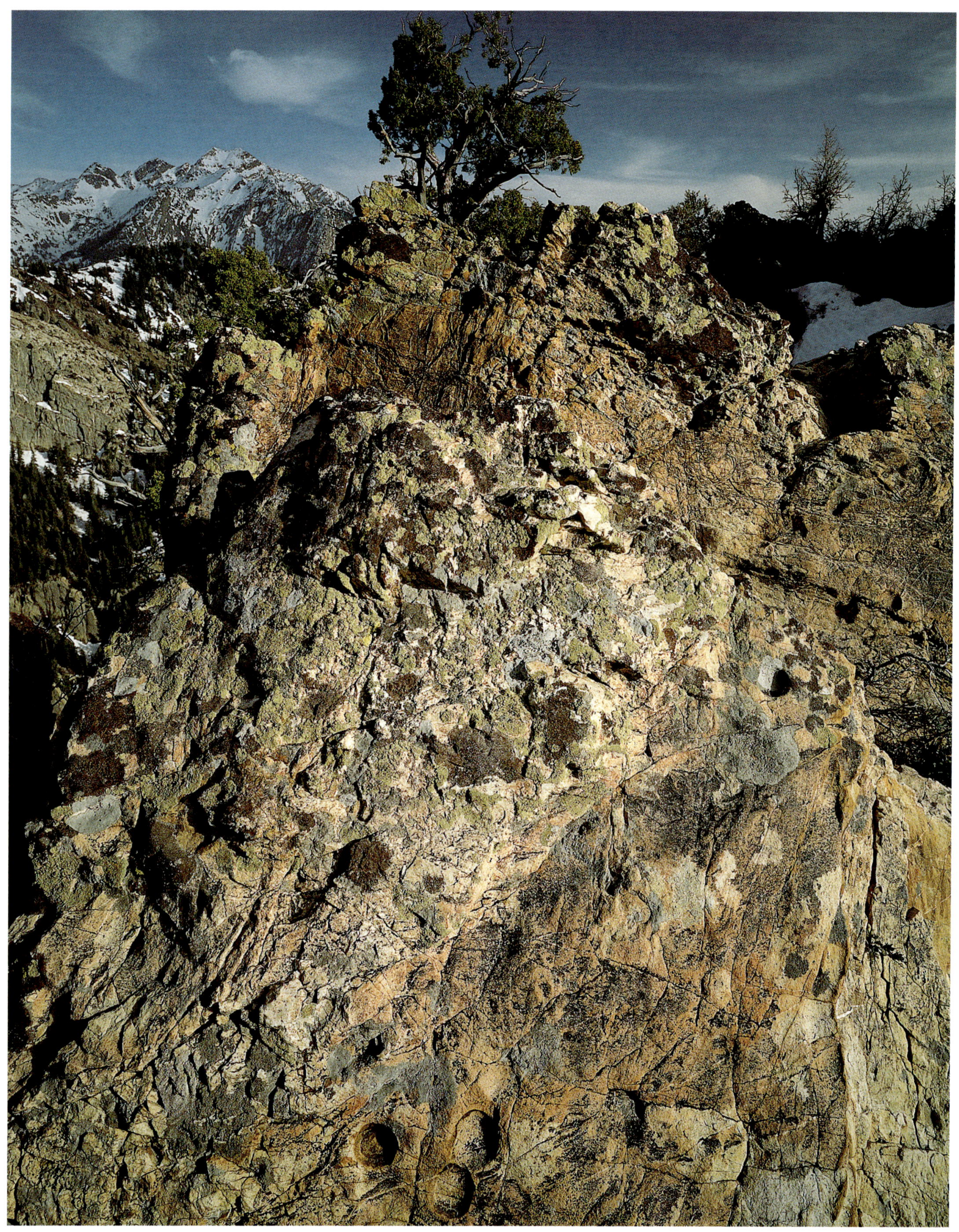

LICHEN-COATED WALL OF MOUNT OLYMPUS, TWIN PEAKS IN THE BACKGROUND, MOUNT OLYMPUS WILDERNESS, WASATCH RANGE.

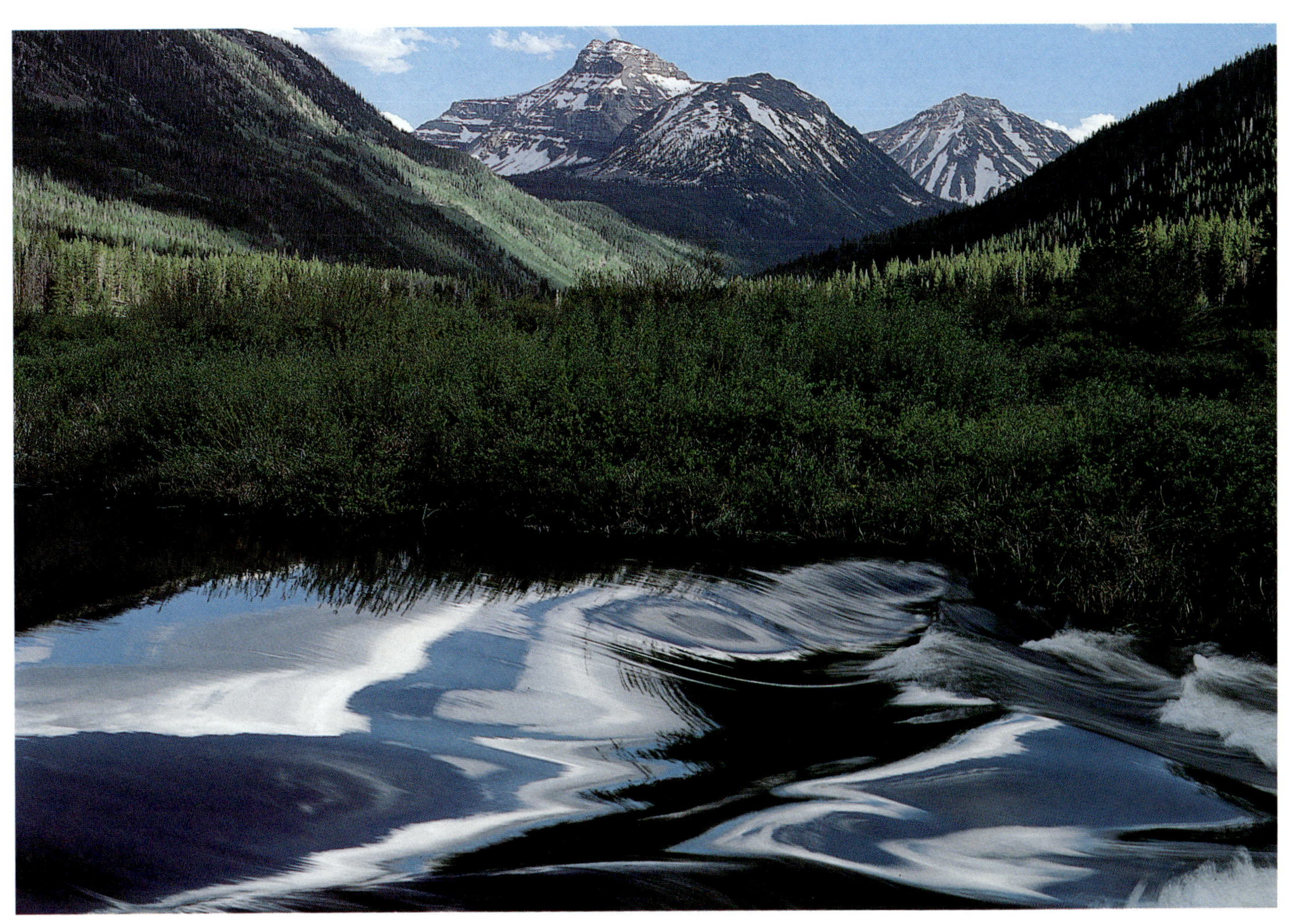

ABOVE: STILLWATER FORK OF BEAR RIVER, HIGH UINTAS WILDERNESS.

FOLLOWING PAGES: A LIGHT MARCH SNOW IN COTTONWOOD CREEK, WASATCH RANGE, ABOVE SALT LAKE CITY.

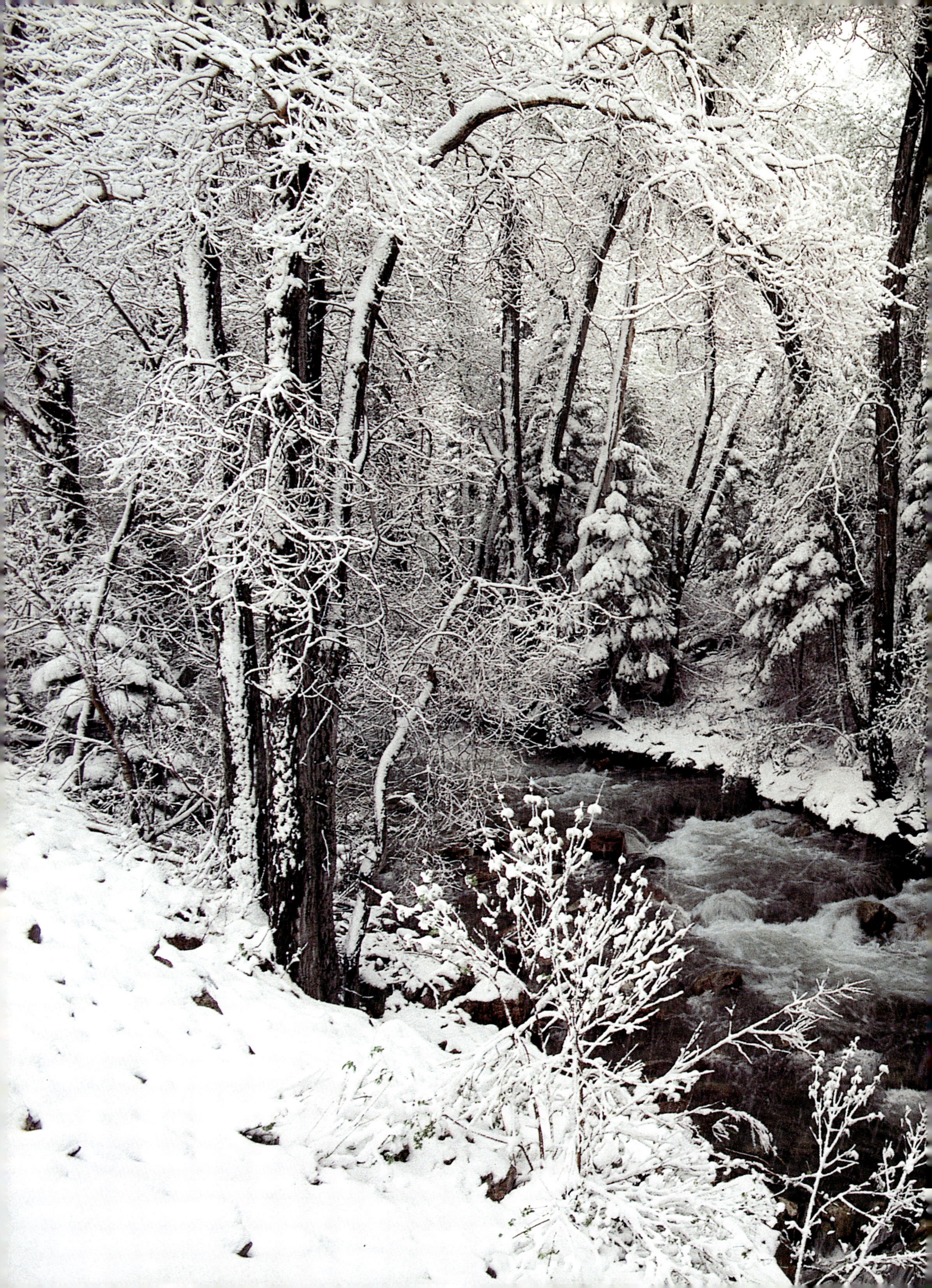

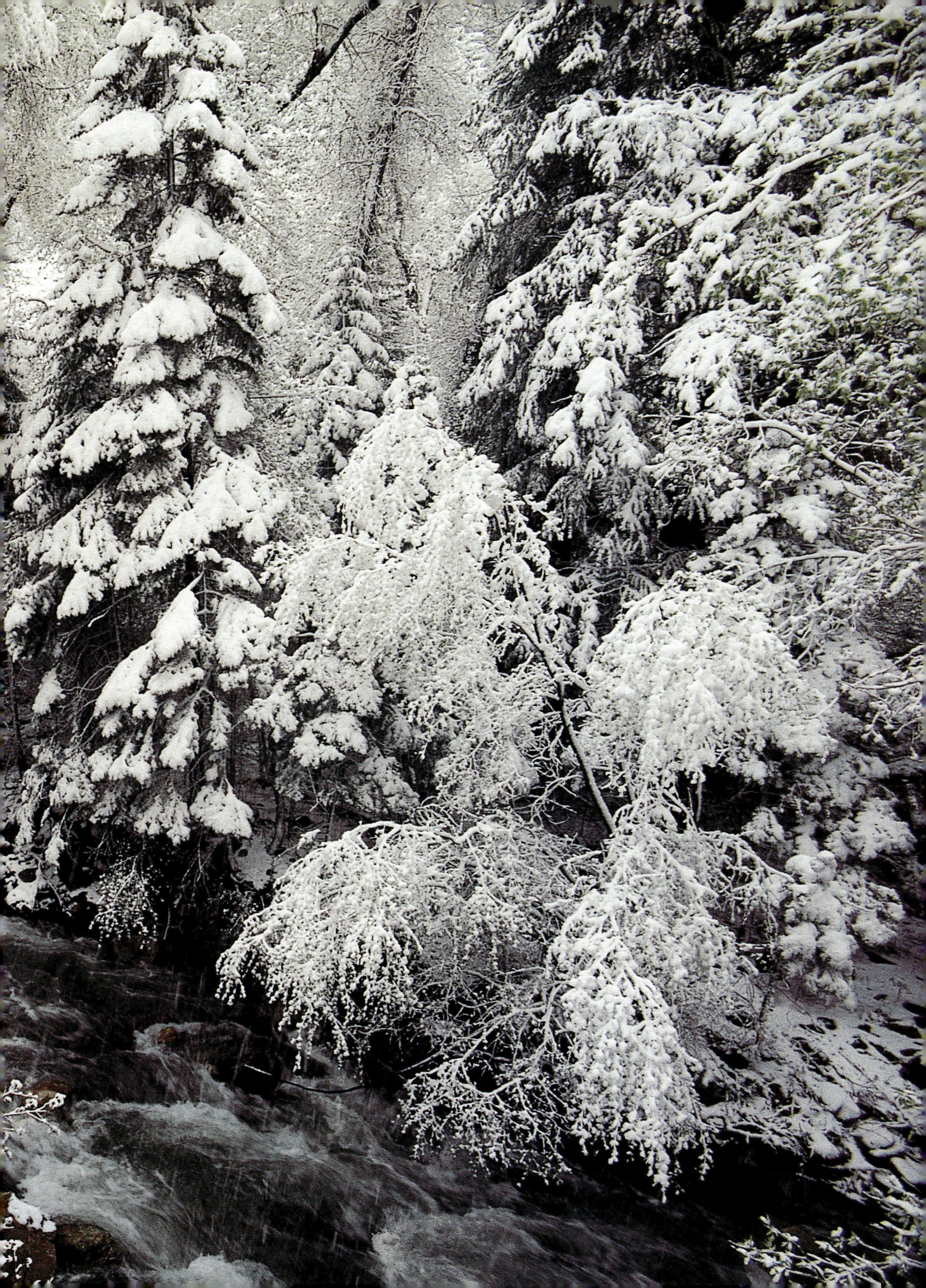

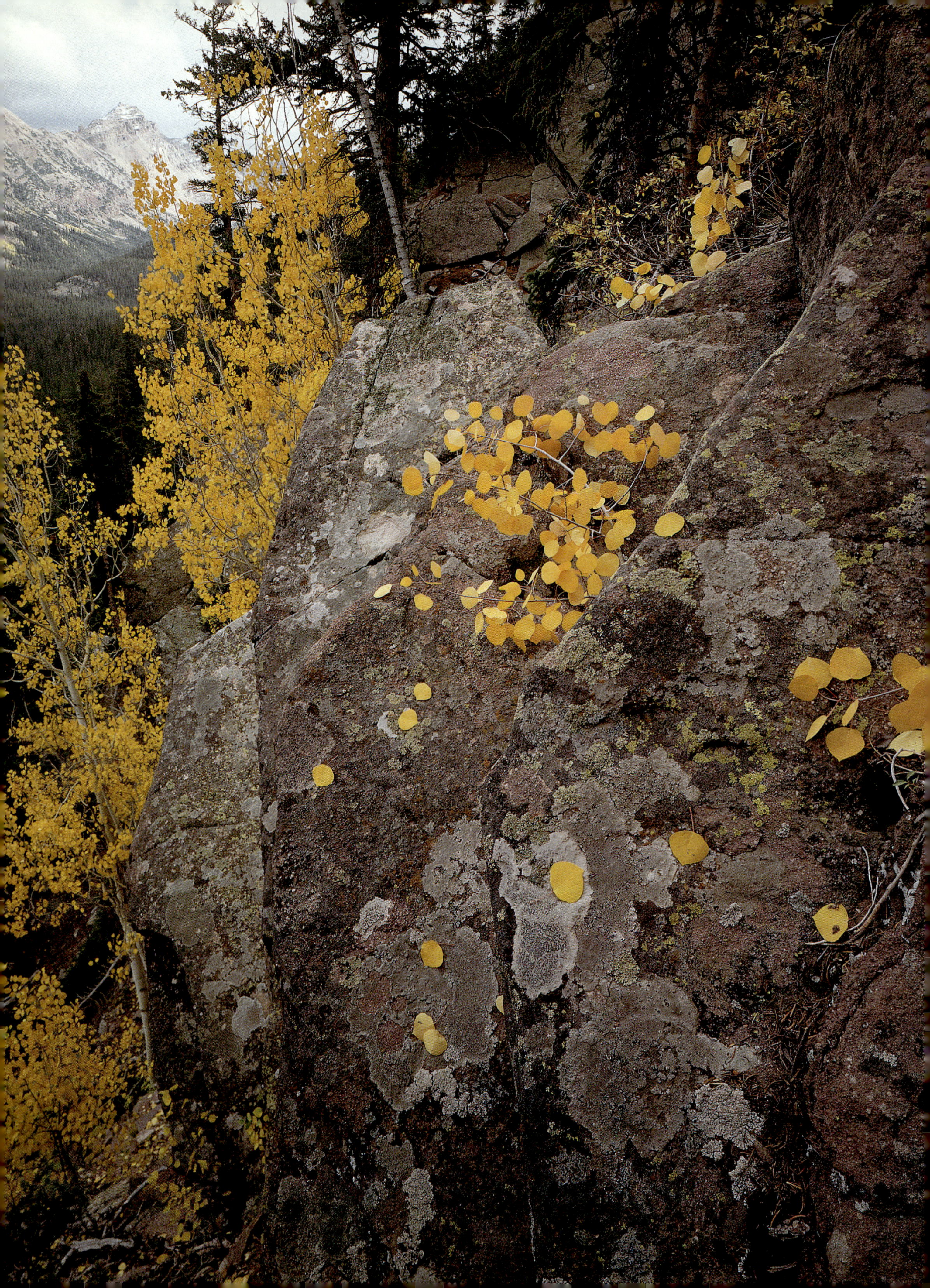

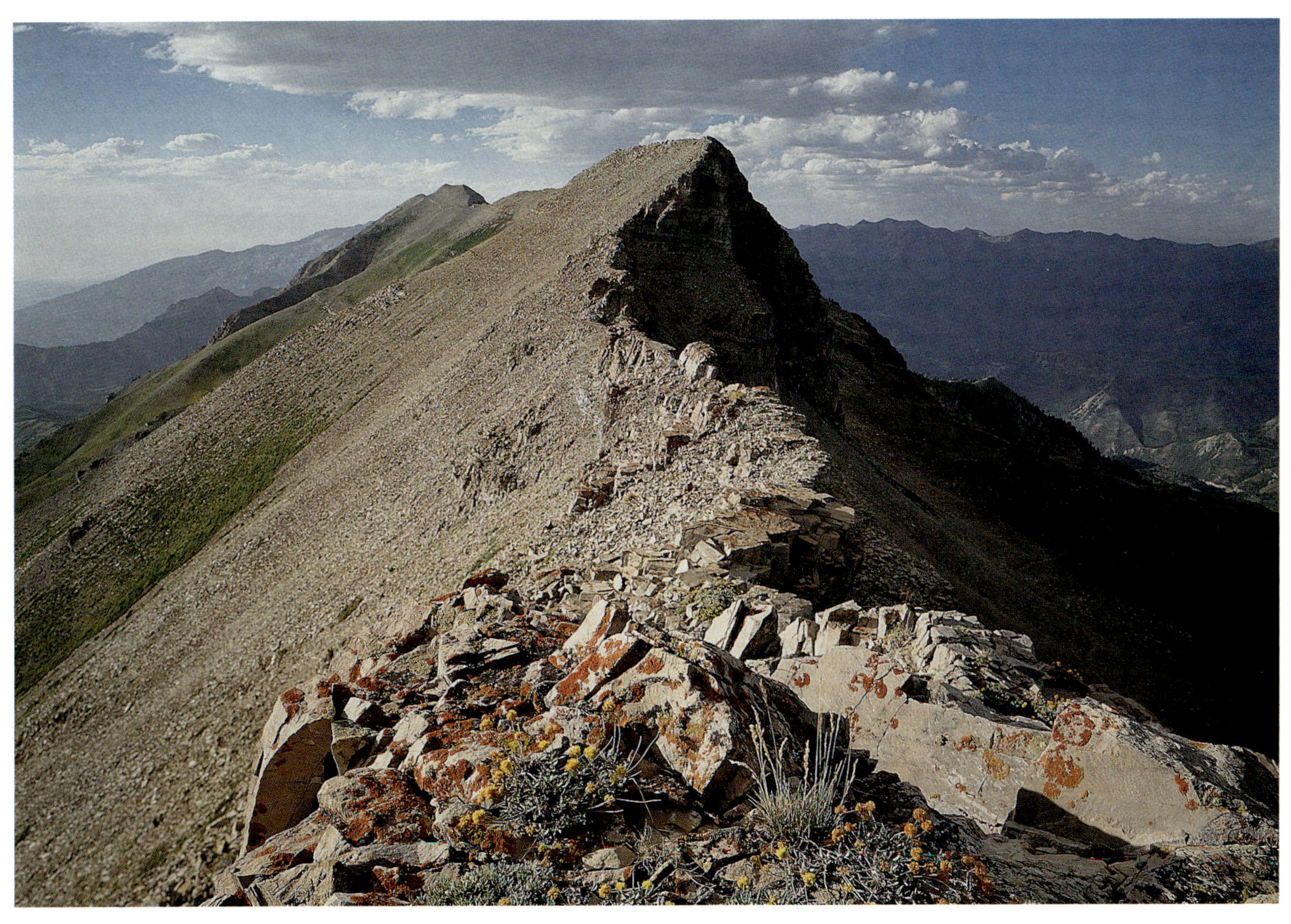

LEFT: EAST FORK OF BEAR RIVER IN THE HIGH UINTAS WILDERNESS.

ABOVE: QUARTZITES ON THE NORTH PEAKS OF MOUNT TIMPANOGOS, MOUNT TIMPANOGOS WILDERNESS.

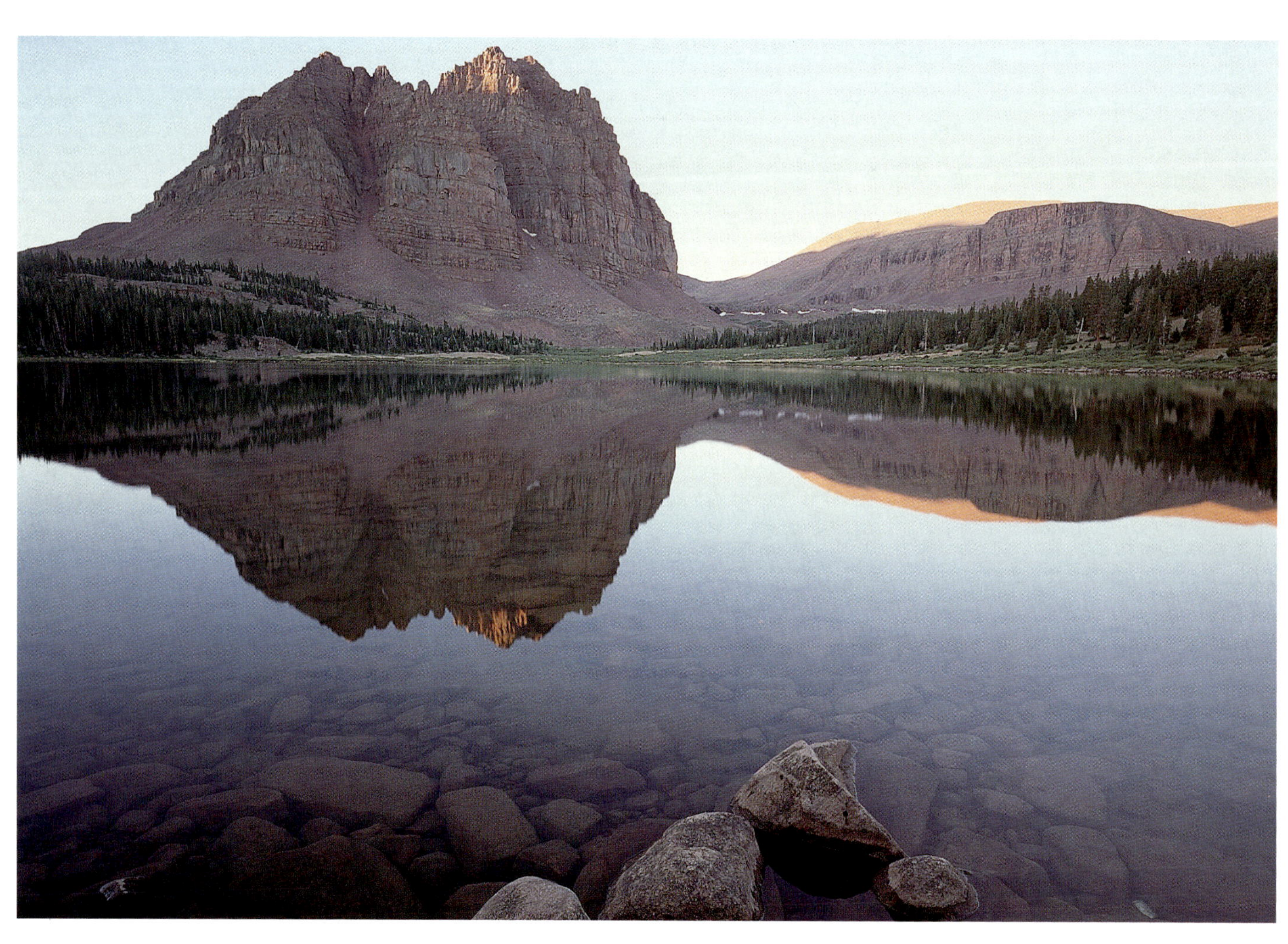

LOWER RED CASTLE LAKE, HIGH UINTAS WILDERNESS.

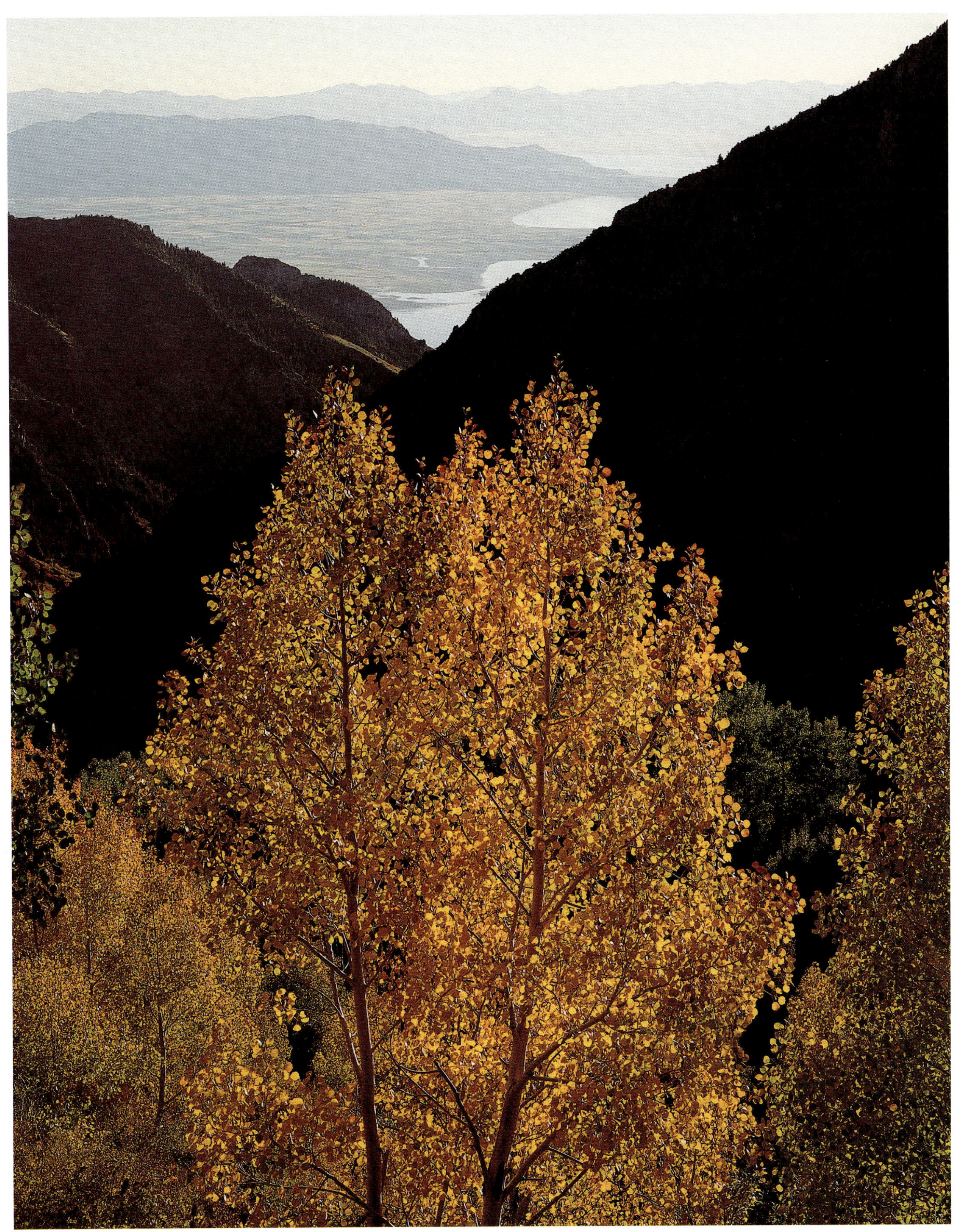

AUTUMN ABOVE UTAH LAKE, WASATCH RANGE.

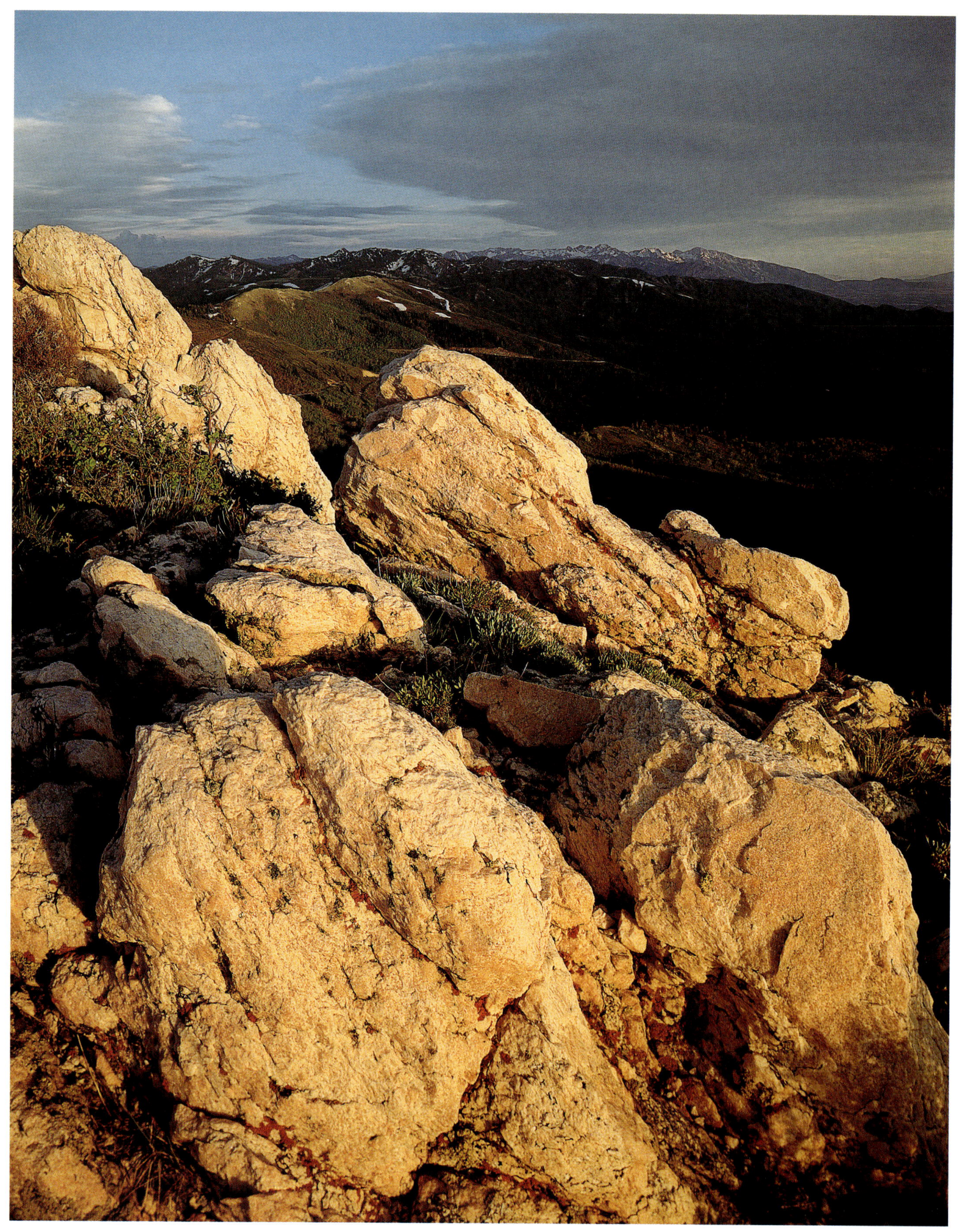

GRANITE OUTCROP, WASATCH RANGE.

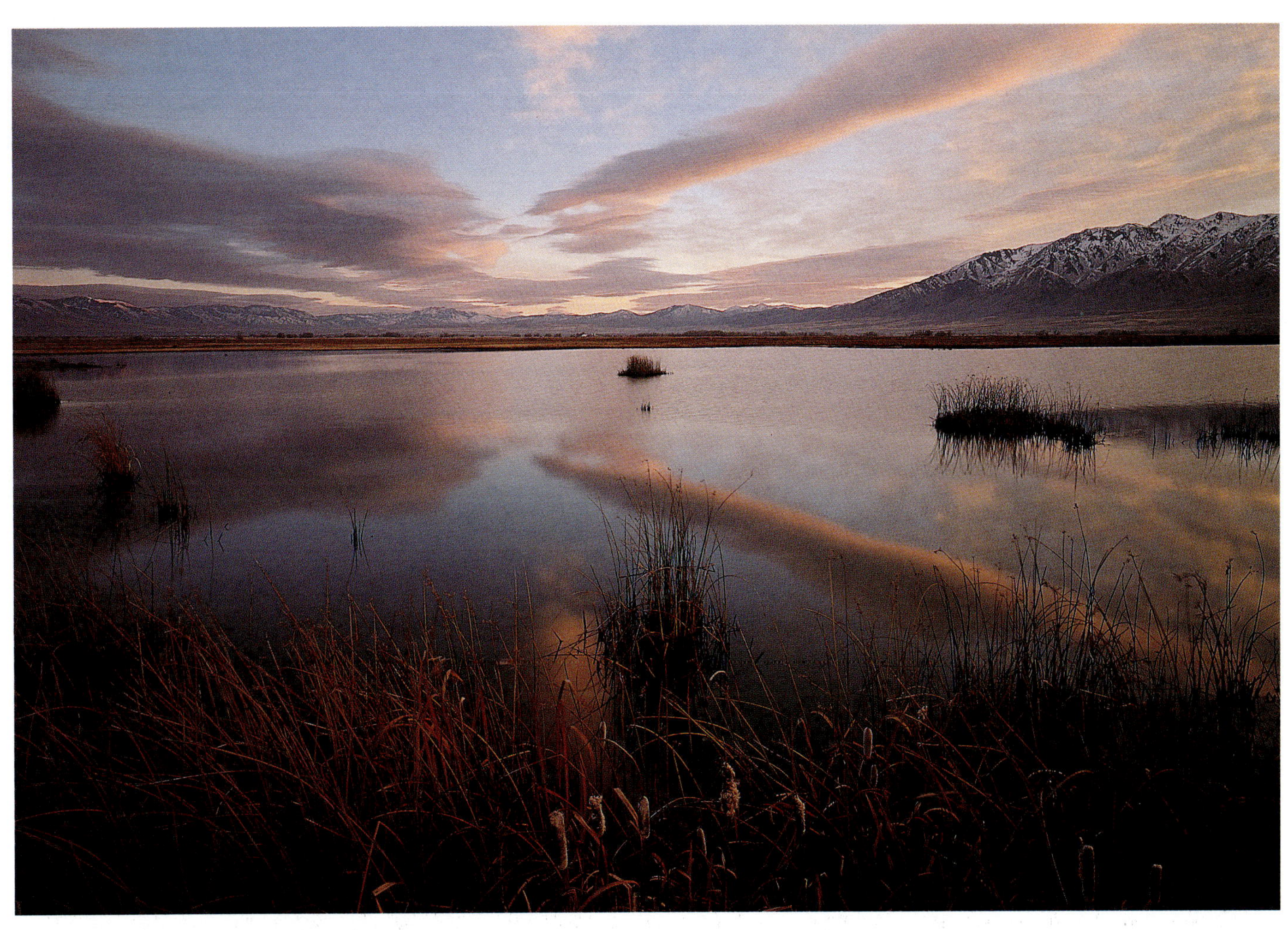

ABOVE: A MARSH ALONG THE LOGAN RIVER IN NOVEMBER,

CACHE COUNTY, WELLSVILLE MOUNTAINS OF THE WASATCH RANGE ABOVE.

FOLLOWING PAGE: INDIAN PAINTBRUSH AND FIREWEED CARPET MEADOWLANDS OF ALBION BASIN, WASATCH RANGE.

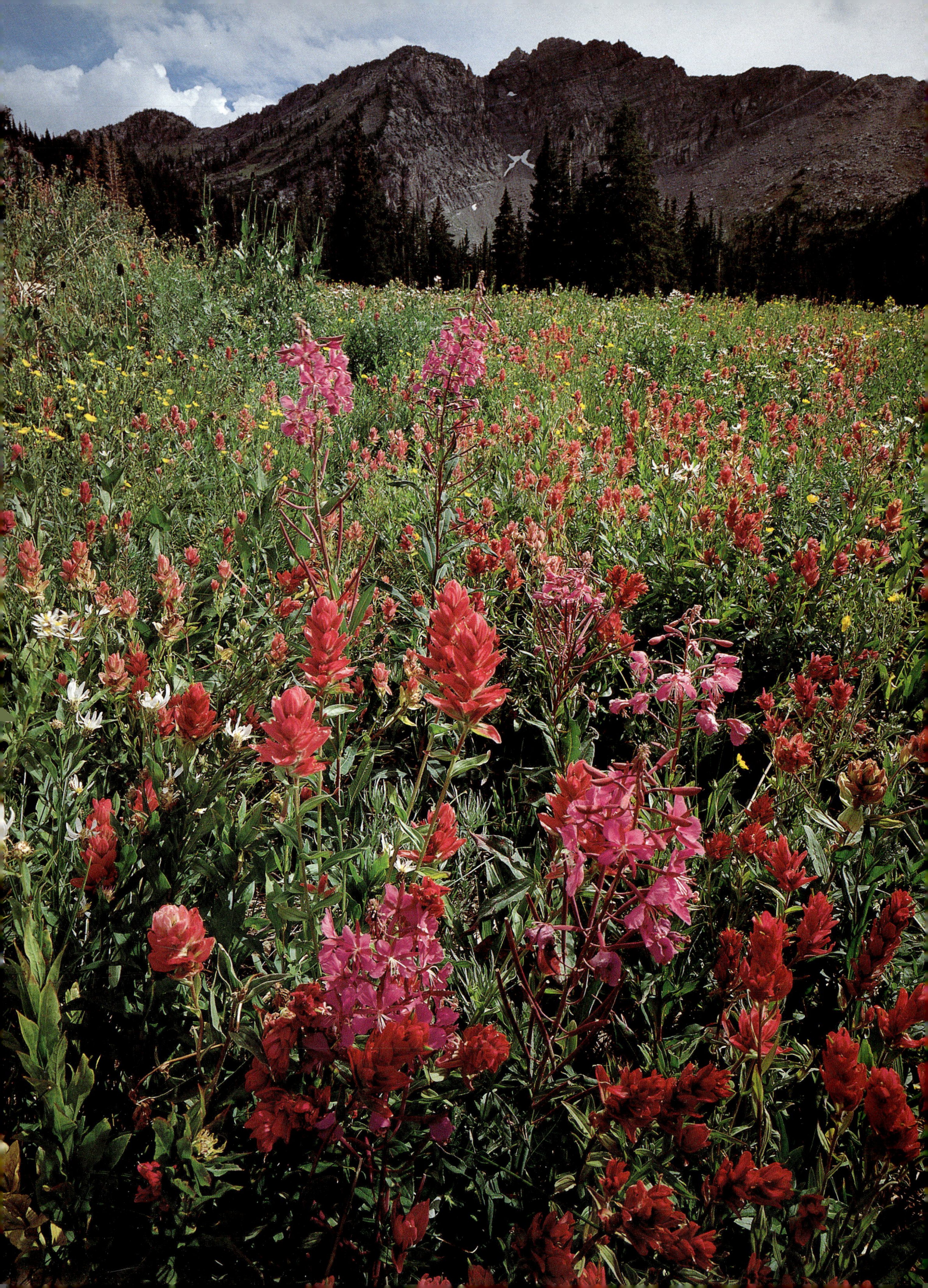